With the humor and love of older siblings, Dakota and Matthew have created the go-to guide and perfect gift for soon-to-be missionaries. *How to Be a Powerful Modern-Day Missionary* is the go-to manual that will not only motivate future missionaries, but also give them real tools to be successful and powerful. It will teach them how to have the grit to endure and show them what makes missions and the gospel fun. If you are a prospective missionary or know someone who is, you need this book.

—Hank Smith, best-selling author and motivational speaker

"I am a mom of six children ages seven through eighteen, and this book got me wishing I was the one serving a full-time mission! I want each of my children to read it! I want to give it to the sister missionaries serving in my ward. I want to give it to every full-time and pre-missionary I know. Seriously, you will too!"

—Lani Hilton, mom of six pre-missionaries and author of *Celebrate Sunday*

"Whether deciding to serve a mission, wanting to be prepared for the challenges and opportunities of missionary service, or seeking to be the best missionary possible, this book will enlighten, guide, and help you thoughtfully and enjoyably prepare. I've already identified five of my grandchildren I plan to give this book to."

—Steven C. Wheelwright, former president of BYU–Hawaii and dean of Harvard Business School

"This fun, quick read will help you be an effective missionary from day one by giving you the tools you need to deal with the most common challenges missionaries face. A must-read for any prospective missionary."

—Brigitte Madrian, dean of BYU Marriott School of Business

"Finally, a book to navigate life as a missionary. So relevant, so timely, and so needed today. Filled with incredible stories, examples, and pictures, this book by Dakota and Matthew shows us how to be powerful and productive missionaries while having fun along the way. A must-read for any current and prospective missionary."

—David M. R. Covey, best-selling author of *The Highly Effective Missionary*

"I wish I had this to prepare for my mission. But I have four more boys who are preparing who will love it!!"

—Chad Lewis, Taiwan Taichung Mission,
BYU and NFL athlete, Super Bowl XXXIV champion

"While it is written by elders, the principles apply equally well to sisters . . . and make it very FUN!"

—Elizabeth Simmons, Singapore mission president's wife , 2015–2018

"After having read this book, I wish I would have served a mission."

—Belton Stant, San Francisco, California

"Easy to read, hard to put down. Insightful, practical advice and an entertaining read as well. Filled with real-life examples, demonstrating that the authors practiced what they are teaching."

— Bradley Mains, Singapore mission president, 2012–2015

"This book discusses things most young missionaries are not aware of. I wish I would have had this resource before I served. I intend to use it with my boys."

—Taysom Hill, BYU and NFL New Orleans Saints quarterback

"I couldn't put this book down. If you're preparing for a mission, read this book. If someone you love is preparing for a mission, get them this book! This book is FABULOUS! I will be getting a copy for my own children and encourage you to do the same! This book can change your mission. Highly recommended!"

—John Hilton III, associate professor of religious studies at BYU Provo, author of *Suit Up* and *The Coming Forth of the Book of Mormon*

"This candid, timely, and readable book is both insightful and inspiring."

—Roger B. Porter, Harvard professor of business and government and former presidential adviser

How to Be a Powerful Modern-Day Missionary is a must-read for youth and young adults considering missionary service and for those preparing for it. It speaks candidly about the challenging aspects of being a missionary and shows how those who prepare and serve in God's way will not only find missionary work to be life-changing, but fun as well.

—Stephen Simmons, Singapore mission president 2015–2018

"An exemplary guide to becoming a powerful missionary in these last, last days."

—Chris Heimerdinger, best-selling author of The Tennis Shoes Adventure series

"I wish I had read this before my mission!"

—More than 100 returned missionaries who have read and enjoyed *How to Be a Powerful Modern-Day Missionary*

HOW TO BE

A POWERFUL MODERN-DAY MISSIONARY

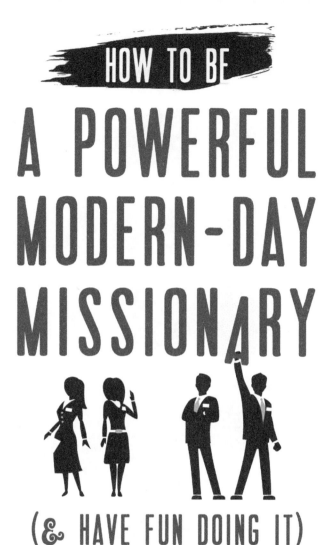

(& HAVE FUN DOING IT)

HOW TO BE
A POWERFUL MODERN-DAY MISSIONARY

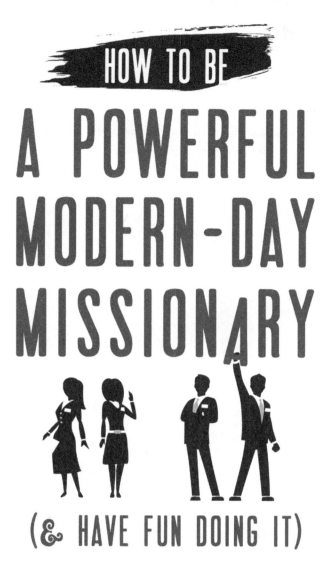

(& HAVE FUN DOING IT)

DAKOTA PIERCE & MATTHEW SPURRIER

CFI
AN IMPRINT OF CEDAR FORT, INC.
SPRINGVILLE, UTAH

All stories in this book are from memory but were sent to those persons described to verify accuracy. We apologize in advance for any discrepancy between our perspectives and God's. Additionally, all names have been changed for privacy.

—Dakota and Matthew

This is not an official publication of The Church of Jesus Christ of Latter-day Saints. The opinions and views expressed herein belong solely to the author and do not necessarily represent the opinions or views of Cedar Fort, Inc. Permission for the use of sources, graphics, and photos is also solely the responsibility of the author.

ISBN 13: 978-1-4621-3703-9

Published by CFI, an imprint of Cedar Fort, Inc.
2373 W. 700 S., Springville, UT 84663
Distributed by Cedar Fort, Inc., www.cedarfort.com

LIBRARY OF CONGRESS CONTROL NUMBER: 2020933666

Cover design by Shawnda T. Craig
Cover design © 2020 Cedar Fort, Inc.

Printed in the United States of America

10 9 8 7 6 5 4 3 2 1

Printed on acid-free paper

FOR FUN . . . WHAT ELSE?

CONTENTS

INTRODUCTION

⟨∽⊙☙⟩

Two years ago, when Matthew and I stumbled into the hot, humid Singapore airport terminal after our twenty-one-hour flight from the missionary training center (MTC), we thought we knew everything there was to know about missionary work. We soon learned that on a scale from "zero" to "knowing everything," we were, unfortunately, much closer to zero. Yes, our teenage selves went to mission prep class. Yes, we spent many weeks in the MTC. Yes, we read our scriptures. And yes, we said our prayers. But looking back, there was so little we knew about what being a missionary in the field actually entailed.

Since then, we have asked ourselves many times, "Why weren't we prepared?" Had we not paid attention in mission prep class? Had we not read our scriptures enough? Were our prayers not sincere? While these are questions of utmost priority, we later realized that they weren't the real reasons we felt unprepared. We were spiritually prepared. We had honest, personal testimonies and desires to be great missionaries. What we lacked was a vision of who great modern-day missionaries are and the mental, emotional, and social skills they must possess.

It's easy to think of great ancient missionary examples. Think of Jonah being swallowed by a whale, Ammon cutting off people's arms, and Joseph Smith being tarred and feathered. It's much harder to imagine them today wearing white shirts and ties while riding bikes or driving cars. Certainly, Ammon and many others' stories would have looked different had they operated under today's standards.

So how can we gain a vision of how Ammon and others would act *today*? And where can we learn the skills they would likely use *now*? Fortunately, they are all found in *Preach My Gospel*. The best thing a teenager preparing for a mission can do is to read and internalize *Preach My Gospel*. All the skills and techniques we talk about are in that book. Plus, it's written by the greatest twenty-first-century missionary examples we have: our living apostles and prophets.

Now, why write another book when *Preach My Gospel* already exists? Well, when we were seventeen years old, we tried what we just suggested—that is, to read and internalize *Preach My Gospel*. Unfortunately, as teenagers, we found it dense and boring, which stemmed from a lack of context. As teenagers, how are we supposed to develop the "faith to find" without actually having tried to find? (See *Preach My Gospel*, "Developing the Faith to Find," page 159.) God's holy prophets and apostles wrote *Preach My Gospel* as a manual for missionaries currently serving, not necessarily for missionaries preparing to serve. Our book's purpose is to break *Preach My Gospel* down into small, applicable bites for preparing missionaries.

For us, it took nearly a full year of missionary service before we could even begin to pinpoint the mental, emotional, and social skills that great modern-day missionaries possess. In other words, we want to save you from spending a year deciphering these skills. We want to give you the jump-start we never had. In doing so, we know that you will bring many more souls unto Christ, develop a stronger testimony of His restored church, and honestly have more *fun*!

Some of you might be thinking, "Well, yes, I want to go on a mission, but is missionary work actually fun? I can think of many things that sound *more* fun." That's okay. When we began our missions, we had those same feelings. So let's ask an easier question. Do you think God has fun doing missionary work? Of course He does. His sole purpose is "to bring to pass the immortality and eternal life of man" (Moses 1:39). And trust us, He's happy doing it. If you think about it, He's been doing it for eternity, so He'd better love it.

When we started our missions, we could have thought of a million things that sounded like more fun than missionary work, but as time passed, we realized we would honestly rather have done missionary work than watched an NBA game, *The Bachelorette*, or anything else. That's not to say that the NBA or *The Bachelorette* got boring. We still enjoy both of them, but missionary work simply became much more interesting, meaningful, and fulfilling.

Don't get us wrong—missions are hard. There may be difficult wards and branches, annoying companions, challenging areas, long transfers, and complicated languages to learn, but hard and fun are not mutually exclusive. They can coexist.

You might be wondering what exactly you're going to learn from this book (besides how to have fun). Instead of randomly picking topics, we took a survey of over six hundred returned missionaries to find out what the hardest part of their mission was. This is what we learned:

What was the Hardest Part of Your Mission?

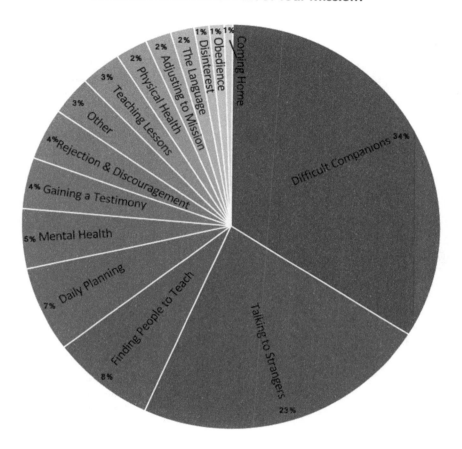

Whether people had difficult companions, felt awkward talking to strangers, struggled with mental or physical health, or didn't know how to teach well, plan well, or gain a testimony, there were many things that were hard throughout their missions. This book will address each of these topics and help you understand what you need *now* to succeed on your mission.

MATTHEW

My time in the MTC was rough. I was the slowest at learning the mission language, my companion didn't like me for a time, and I was still figuring out why I was there. Then, when I got to the mission field, I thought that my first area was a "hard area," and I became frustrated with God. I was working hard but not seeing success.

DAKOTA

The entire first year of my mission seemed hard. I had spent seven months with the same companion, and, similar to Gordon B. Hinckley, I wrote a letter home that said, "Dear Dad, This is so hard . . . it's just really, really hard." Just like Gordon B. Hinckley had felt, I wasn't sure I belonged on a mission. I was sick of it (Sheri L. Dew, "The 2 Sentences That Changed President Gordon B. Hinckley's Life Forever," *LDS Living*).

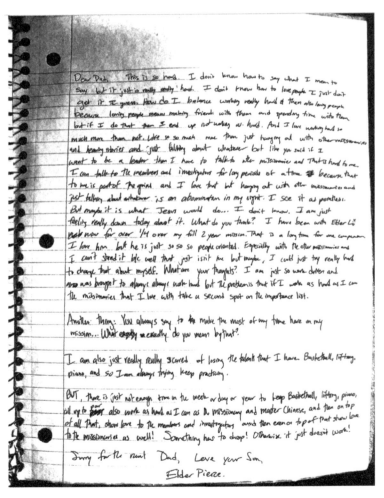

Dakota's original letter to his dad

So, how did we get from that point to here and now, writing a book about how much fun missionary work is? How did we make such a 180-degree turn?

It doesn't matter. If we told you that answer, we'd be bad teachers. Great teachers don't *give* people fish. They teach them *how* to fish. They teach them *why* we fish.

President Boyd K. Packer once asked a man to explain how salt tasted.

"Well-I-uh, it is not sweet and it is not sour," the man ventured.

After several attempts, the man ultimately gave up attempting to describe how salt tasted. ("The Candle of the Lord," from a talk given at a seminar for new mission presidents, June 25, 1982. See churchofjesuschrist.org/study/ensign/1983/01/the-candle-of-the-lord.title2?lang=eng#title2.)

Just as the taste of salt is more difficult to *describe* than *recognize*, we want you to experience missionary work at its most meaningful levels rather than be able to describe it. This means, however, that you will need to put forth effort. Reading our book will give you the beginning tools and context you need to succeed as a missionary, but learning *why* and *how* missionary work is fun requires you to actually do missionary work.

To help you start *experiencing* missionary work, we have included a challenge at the end of each chapter. Some will be more difficult than others, but we *know* from experience that miracles will flow if you attempt them with real intent and sincere effort.

Instead of trying to come up with a one-sentence thesis statement to explain why we now have so much fun doing missionary work, we want to help you create your own thesis statement. By the end of this book, we want you to know why missionary work is fun according to you—not us.

We're not the only ones who want you to know this for yourself. Modern prophets have said,

> Dear Fellow [future] Missionary:
>
> . . . There is no more compelling work than this, nor any which brings greater satisfaction.
>
> . . . More happiness awaits you than you have ever experienced as you labor among His children.
>
> The First Presidency
>
> (See *Preach My Gospel*, v.)

Think about that for a second. "More happiness awaits you than you have *ever* experienced." So why do people shy away from missionary work? Is it too uncomfortable? Is any small amount of discomfort or awkwardness worth more happiness "than you have ever experienced?"

You are going to have real fun helping God's children come unto Christ. God's children aren't mere mortals but rather potential future gods and goddesses that will rule worlds (see *The Weight of Glory*, C. S. Lewis, 45–46). Each day you have the opportunity to change peoples' lives. LET'S DO IT!

CHAPTER 1
KNOW YOUR WHY

MANY OF YOU MIGHT BE LIKE MATTHEW

1. You grew up in Utah, and most of your friends and high school classmates were members of the Church.
2. Most of your life you have believed the Church is true because it teaches good standards and principles. Serving a mission just seems like the next logical thing to do, especially since all your friends are serving too.
3. You are still working on cementing your testimony and moving from believing to knowing.

OTHERS OF YOU MIGHT BE LIKE DAKOTA

1. You grew up outside of Utah, have extended family with mixed opinions about the Church, and are feeling both the pressure to serve and not to serve.
2. You have a once-in-a-lifetime opportunity (mine was college sports, but yours might be music, school, work, marriage, etc.) and are hearing "a mission isn't for everyone" voices from every which way.
3. No one in your family has ever served a mission, so you have no idea what to expect.

Looking back, our teenage doubts and fears now appear minuscule when compared to the blessings we received from serving. Not going would have been the biggest mistake of our lives. However, if you are still not sure about going on a mission—or before you go just because you are "supposed to"—we have one suggestion:

KNOW *YOUR* WHY

No one wants to listen to or be converted by an eighteen-year-old who says, "You should join the Church because my mom knows it's true." That's not *your* why. *The best missionaries go on their missions with honest, personal testimonies.* There are many different ways to gain a testimony, and everyone's spiritual journey is unique. However, if you want a formula that we know works every time, then read the Book of Mormon and sincerely ask God if it's true. In other words, test Moroni's promise:

> And when ye shall receive these things [the Book of Mormon], I would exhort you that ye would ask God, the Eternal Father, in the name of Christ, if these things are not true; and if ye shall ask with a sincere heart, with real intent, having faith in Christ, he will manifest the truth of it unto you, by the power of the Holy Ghost.
>
> And by the power of the Holy Ghost ye may know the truth of all things. (Moroni 10:4–5)

At this point in your life, you have probably spent many hours in Sunday School and seminary classes listening to youth leaders and teachers repeatedly beg you to put Moroni's promise to the test. To appease their nagging, you may have even lamely tried it, but gaining a personal witness takes more than half trying. It takes your real try, and often even more. Think of Enos. He prayed all day and into the night before the Lord answered his prayer (Enos 1:4–5). Don't read five pages of 1 Nephi, give a five-minute prayer, and then wonder what you did wrong when you don't see an angel. God needs to see your *real* try, because, contrary to intuition, faith does not flow from miracles but rather precedes them (see "Miracles," Bible Dictionary).

DAKOTA

I had just graduated high school and was preparing for my freshman basketball season at MIT. I knew I needed to talk to my coach soon about the whole mission thing (*if* I was going to go), and that conversation was going to be far from easy. Our team needed a point guard, and I was it.

MIT Varsity Basketball Team; Dakota is pictured front row, far right, #23

My dad said that serving a mission was totally up to me, but because he is a sports fanatic and a convert who didn't serve a mission, I felt he was partial to me staying in school and playing ball. Plus, considering my responsibility to the basketball team, I knew I would sound like an idiot if I went and told my coach I was going to serve a two-year mission for a church that my mom believed was true.

As I was pondering my options, I remembered Moroni's promise, which my seminary teachers had practically beaten over my head. I had prayed many times about the Church and the Book of Mormon but never really received a tangible answer. As much as receiving an answer to a prayer still seemed like a foreign concept, I realized then that I *needed* a testimony. I *needed* to know if the Church was true. Otherwise, having to deal with expectations from my dad, my extended family, and my basketball team seemed impossible. And besides, if the Church wasn't true, what was the point of going on a mission? I had to know.

That night, I decided I would put all my effort into reading the Book of Mormon in seven days. I would fast the first day and then again seven days later, and I would pray before and after reading each day. I thought that if the Church was true, I would get some miraculous answer on day seven after I fasted the second time. If not, then I guessed that would be that.

It was summer, and besides going on a few dates and preparing for the upcoming basketball season, I had a ton of time on my hands. I remember working out in the morning until around noon and then coming home and reading the Book of Mormon in my bedroom from about 1:00 to 7:00 p.m. each day. Back in seminary, I had half-heartedly read the Book of Mormon as a graduation requirement and remembered it felt like a chore. At first, I thought this time was going to feel the same—and, indeed, it began that way. However, by the end of my first day of reading, I was genuinely enjoying the Book of Mormon.

As the week went on, the peace and clarity I felt was unmistakable. By day four, it was as if I had found renewed purpose in my life. Still, I was looking forward to day seven when I thought I would receive some miraculous witness of the Book of Mormon after completing my weeklong experiment. At the end of the week, after fasting a second time, nothing miraculous occurred. No angels appeared. No fire fell from the sky. But that didn't matter. On day seven, I wrote in my journal:

> I read the Book of Mormon in one week. Although I did not get the answer I thought I was going to get . . . I received the Spirit in a different way. While reading throughout the week, I have felt a renewed sense of peace and happiness that I have never felt before. I want to serve the Lord for the rest of my life. I want to teach others about the Book of Mormon . . . Go on a life-long mission? Forget two years. (July 23, 2013)

And teach others about the Book of Mormon was exactly what I did! I didn't need to wait to be a full-time missionary, nor did I want to. From that week on, I began to instinctively reach far beyond my previous comfort zone to share the gospel. As a normal teenage member of the Church, I went from being relatively shy about my beliefs to proactively giving out copies of the Book of Mormon on airplanes and inviting both friends and strangers to church. *Preach My Gospel* teaches, "A great indicator of one's personal conversion is the desire to share the gospel with others" (page 13). The truth is, missionary work comes naturally when you have an honest testimony.

Plain and simple, the desire to do missionary work is something we can't teach you. That is something you need to gain from God through spiritual experiences. So if that's something you still need, then put this book down and go get a testimony. President James E. Faust taught, "You cannot convert people beyond your own conversion" ("What I Want My Son to Know before He Leaves on His Mission," *Ensign*, May 1996).

There is a reason why, when you are on an airplane and the air pressure is too low, that they tell you to put the oxygen mask on yourself first before helping others. (See "Why You're Instructed to Put Oxygen Masks on Yourself First," HuffPost.) There is a reason why Jesus Christ went to pray in far-off places for long periods of time when He could have been out serving others (Luke 6:12; Mark 1:35). We all, including the Savior, need to spend time and energy connecting with God to have those sacred spiritual experiences that will carry us through our missions and lives.

Now some of you might be thinking, "Well, it's easy for you two to say 'go on a mission!' since you both had strong testimonies before going."

MATTHEW

While I had the beginnings of a testimony before my mission, taking the Book of Mormon seriously on my mission is what cemented my conviction and drive for the gospel. Before leaving *on* my mission, I was in a band called Solarsuit, with four other members of the Church who were talking about potentially staying home from their missions (at least for a while) to continue their music careers. We weren't just "some high school band." We were actually good. We had played with bands like Imagine Dragons, Capital Cities, Panic! at the Disco, Blue October, and more, and we were rated in the Top Five Up and Coming Bands in Utah (*Salt Lake City Weekly*, "Solarsuit").

Solarsuit band, left to right, Porter, Luke, Matthew, Ethan, and Logan

Although I always had the idea that I should serve a mission, there was a part of me that wasn't sure. In high school, I read the Book of Mormon at youth conference (as part of an assignment) and felt that my answer was to "go on a mission," but I didn't get much more than that. With this flicker of an answer illuminating only one step forward, I decided to serve a mission. Only after entering the MTC did I truly solidify my testimony. There I remember reading the Book of Mormon a second time to test Moroni's promise. I thought, "Woah, this stuff is GOLD." As I read, I prayed wholeheartedly, and that time it felt like God wrapped His arms around me and said, "Welcome home." It was there, in the MTC, that I came to know that the Book of Mormon was true.

Joseph Smith taught, "Take away the Book of Mormon . . . and where is our religion? We have none" (*History of the Church*, 2:52). Throughout my mission, with the Book of Mormon as my keystone, other doctrines such as the restoration of the priesthood, temple ordinances, modern-day prophets, and Christ's Atonement all seemed to fall into place as I studied them. That's not to say that gaining a testimony of those other doctrines was easy (it took real effort too!), but the stage was set, the context lit, and my faith set on fire.

NOT "WHY WE BELIEVE"

Joseph Smith translated more scripture than the entire New Testament in less than sixty-five working days, and in the space of a few years he "established an organization which . . . has withstood every adversity and is as effective today in governing a worldwide membership [of millions] . . . as it was in governing a membership of 300 in 1830" (*Teachings of Presidents of the Church: Joseph Smith*, 551–52). The natural man finds these facts impressive. However, facts are not *why* we believe. The Apostle Paul writes, "The natural man receiveth not the things of the Spirit of God; for they are foolishness unto him; neither can he know them, because they are spiritually discerned" (1 Corinthians 2:14). Many learned scholars have praised the Book of Mormon for its literary prowess, yet they still don't believe.

Your *why* must consist of spiritual knowledge gained through communication with your Father in Heaven. There is no other way.

Many people who serve missions come back with mature planning skills, more effective goal-setting methods, and powerful stress-management techniques. Many people go on missions in hopes of learning a new language or experiencing a new culture. You will inevitably learn and gain most, if not all, of these skills and experiences, but that's not *why* we go on missions. We go because Jesus Christ died for us and lives again. We go because He asked us to (see Matthew 28:19). We go because the gospel has been restored, and Christ is coming again! We go because, like Ammon and the sons of Mosiah, we hope to be "instruments in his hands" to bring if but "some soul" unto the feet of Christ, to taste of that fruit which is "desirable above all other fruit" (see Alma 26:15, 30; 1 Nephi 8:12).

The catch is, you need to taste that fruit first before you can ever hope to have any *fun* sharing it. Taste that fruit by testing Moroni's promise. Read the Book of Mormon and sincerely pray to know if it's true. "As a missionary, *you* must first have a personal testimony that the Book of Mormon is true" (*Preach My Gospel*, 103; emphasis added).

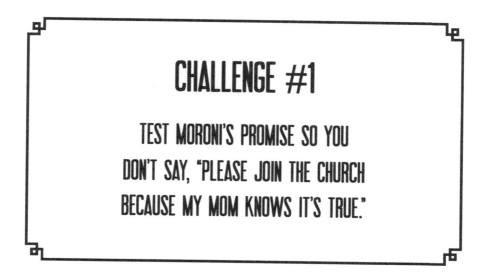

CHALLENGE #1

TEST MORONI'S PROMISE SO YOU DON'T SAY, "PLEASE JOIN THE CHURCH BECAUSE MY MOM KNOWS IT'S TRUE."

HELPFUL SUGGESTIONS

- Read the Book of Mormon and test Moroni's promise by sincerely praying to know if it's true. Think about what "sincerely" means for you. For Dakota, it meant fasting as well.
- Read *Preach My Gospel*, chapter 4, the section called "Learn to Recognize the Promptings of the Spirit," and Alma 32. Record in your journal how you receive answers to specific prayers.
- Ask friends and family why they served missions and how they got their testimony.

PLEASE MESSAGE US WITH QUESTIONS OR SUCCESS STORIES.
EMAIL: THEMODERNDAYMISSIONARIES@GMAIL.COM
INSTAGRAM: @MODERNDAYMISSIONARIES
FACEBOOK: @MODERNDAYMISSIONARIES

CHAPTER 2
OBEDIENCE ENABLES US

We could try to tell you that obedience is fun. In fact, that used to be the title of this chapter. But in our experience, that isn't always the case. Obedience is challenging and can initially seem difficult, unrewarding, or even boring.

Some people might always find the act of obedience "fun." We have not. Rather, we have found that obedience *enables* us to have fun. For instance, we aren't going to claim you should have "fun" getting up at 6:30 a.m. every morning during your mission (although it's great if you do). We will tell you, however, that going to bed early and getting up early will enable you to have more energy and fun throughout the day than you would have otherwise. Our obedience to God qualifies us to receive His power to become far more than we could on our own.

This chapter is laid out to help you first understand what the missionary rules are and why we have them; second, make you aware of the general patterns of disobedience; and third, teach you how to inspire obedience in those around you.

WHAT ARE THE MISSIONARY RULES AND WHY DO WE HAVE THEM?

First of all, what does being obedient mean for a missionary? Well, a mission requires extra standards that are above and beyond the normal commandments you learned as a kid, and they are all found in a little book called *Missionary Standards for Disciples of Jesus Christ*.

Some of the most well-known and commonly disobeyed standards are

- You can't surf the internet, play video games, or watch TV (*Missionary Standards*, 3.6.3).

- You must stay within sight and sound of your companion 24/7, except in the bathroom (*Missionary Standards*, 2.2.2).

- You should follow a structured daily schedule set by your mission president; generally wake up at 6:30 a.m. and sleep at 10:30 p.m. (*Missionary Handbook*, 2.4.2).

- You should always do your best to be doing the Lord's work; in other words, you shouldn't waste time (*Missionary Standards*, 2.1).

SO WHY HAVE RULES?

The First Presidency states, "[These missionary standards] will help protect you physically, spiritually, and emotionally and help you be the disciple Jesus Christ needs you to become" (*Missionary Standards*, "Message from the First Presidency and Quorum of the Twelve Apostles," 3).

From ancient times until today, many people have believed that religion and its rules exist only to keep people "in check" or to control the masses. They believe that religion and its rules "will keep [them] down to be servants." The secular view of the world is that living without God's commandments will set them free. (See Helaman 16:21.)

However, religion and its rules do more than just keep us "in check." If all that missionary rules do for you is to neutralize your secular behavior, then you aren't absorbing the real meaning behind the standards. The rules are there to bring us closer to God and to facilitate a more intimate, interactive relationship with Him. They are there to *enable* us to become like Him.

The issue is, people and missionaries will often find themselves following a secular definition of the commandments while professing faithful intentions. Many missionaries, although perfectly obedient, may reach a point where they feel farther from God than they would like to be. Perhaps they are going through the motions. "Perhaps they have settled for following rules instead of following the Savior" (Brad Wilcox, *The 7-Day Christian*, 789).

With respect to the Law of Moses (the "rules" of ancient days), Jesus taught, "And to love [God] with all the heart, and with all the understanding, and with all the soul, and with all the strength, and to love his neighbor as himself, is more than all whole burnt offerings and sacrifices" (Mark 12:33), or in modern-day terms, "more than all the missionary standards or rules." In fact, "what need of the [commandments] could there be if mankind would obey the first and great and all-embracing commandment?" (James E. Talmage, *Jesus the Christ*, 551).

15

WAIT, MISSIONARIES AREN'T PERFECT?

We remember admiring missionaries as young men and thinking they could do no wrong. We figured every single missionary was working their hardest, following all the rules, and having a ton of fun. The truth is, not all missionaries are exactly obedient. Despite what everyone says and thinks, some missionaries can be disobedient.

Elder Brent H. Nielsen of the Seventy once came to our mission and asked us, "What do you think Satan's greatest temptation is for missionaries?" We looked at him blankly. "Hmmm, pornography?" we asked with uncertainty. "No," he said. "Actually, Satan's greatest temptation for missionaries is to *do nothing.*" If Satan can get you to do nothing, he has just taken one of God's consecrated servants from the playing field. Satan knows there are specific people you are supposed to find, teach, and baptize. By getting you to do nothing, Satan has succeeded in slowing God's work.

We often see a common plotline among disobedient companions. Whether they are junior companions, senior companions, trainers, district leaders, zone leaders, sister training leaders, or assistants to the mission president, the story generally goes something like this:

> My companion seemed fine to start. The first day they woke up on time but took a long shower and got to personal study five minutes late. The second day they got there fifteen minutes late and were still in their pajamas. The third day they didn't make it to personal study. Most likely, they accidentally fell back asleep after the alarm went off. By the end of the first month, sleeping in had become the norm.

No one goes on a mission thinking, "I'm going to be a lazy missionary." No one goes thinking, "I'm going to wake up at noon every day." But it still happens.

An old fable relates how a frog fell into a pot of boiling water. Realizing how hot it was, the frog immediately jumped out. A second frog fell into a cool pot of water. The cool water was then slowly heated to boiling. The second frog didn't notice the increase in temperature and stayed in the water until it was too late, letting itself boil to death (Moral Stories, moralstories.org/frog-hot-water).

No matter how obedient or strong you think you are, this pattern of incremental disobedience can still happen to you, and by the time you realize it, you might have already messed up.

DAKOTA

When I started my mission, I planned to be as obedient as possible. I arrived in my first area in the jungle of Malaysia ready to serve God with everything I had. There I lived with my trainer and two other elders. At first, things seemed okay. Everyone was waking up on time and being productive. However, as the days went on, bit by bit the other elders started sleeping through their alarms. Then they slept through their exercise time and sometimes even their studies. By week three, hidden personal smartphones and DVD players had come out of suitcases. Things happened so subtly that I didn't really think to do anything about it. I soon caught myself sleeping in a couple of times. By week five, the elders were blasting rap music (claiming that it was for language study) and having other missionaries sleep over for game nights. I even found myself staying up a few times far past our curfew and joining in on their games. By week seven, we all were becoming accustomed to playing daily three-hour board games.

Now, if you told me before my mission that in my first area I would be living with elders who would watch movies, blast rap music, sleep in until 10:00 a.m., and play board games for hours every day, I would've said, "No way! I would never let that happen. I would tell the mission president and stand up for what's right." However, it all happened so subtly. I was just like the frog. The rising temperature never registered until it was too late.

I remember feeling disappointed, not only with the missionary force as a whole—realizing that my belief that all missionaries are obedient was false—but also with myself, because despite all my righteous intentions, I had been lured into participating in their shenanigans.

It wasn't that playing board games and staying up late wasn't fun; rather, that that kind of fun only lasted the night. By not following the standards set for missionaries, I lost the Spirit and many opportunities to serve the people of Malaysia.

Often in regard to missionary rules, it isn't a matter of good versus bad. It's a choice between good, better, or best. There is nothing wrong with playing board games, staying up late, or sleeping in. None of these things make you a bad person. They just hold you back from being the best tool in the Lord's hands that you can be. That's why modern-day prophets set these standards. They *enable* missionaries to have a more lasting fun—the type that lasts far beyond an extra few hours of sleep.

Dakota, far right, with a few members and the elders from his house

HOW DO I INSPIRE OBEDIENCE?

Now that you understand what obedience looks like and why it's crucial, we can get to the juiciest part of this chapter. When faced with a questionable situation or disobedient companion, how should you respond? How do you stand for what is right and inspire obedience and faith in those around you?

In reality, there is no one-size-fits-all answer to this. Each situation and companion is unique, and Christlike actions can appear in a variety of ways. So instead of pretending to offer a formula that works every time, we'd like to suggest four principles that have worked for us and others in sticky situations.

1. LOVE THE LORD

It's easy to fall into the trap of thinking that missionary work is a popularity contest. It can seem like the most "popular" missionaries have the most success because, on the outset, that often can be true.

"Popular" missionaries tend to be focused on doing and saying what others want to hear, rather than pleasing God. Think about all the "popular" missionaries in the Book of Mormon: Korihor, who rationalized that "whatsoever a man did was no crime"; Nehor, who taught that church leaders "ought to become popular"; and Sherem, who reasoned that men "cannot tell of things to come" (Alma 30:17; Alma 1:3; Jacob 7:7). Each of them led "away the hearts of many" (Alma 30:18; Alma 1:5; Jacob 7:3). In terms of converting large numbers of people in a short amount of time, Korihor, Nehor, and Sherem were some of the most successful missionaries in the entire Book of Mormon. In truth, disobedient missionaries can have success, though their success is not generally long-lived.

Now think of Alma. Against the powerful King Noah, Alma took an unpopular stance by supporting Abinadi's teachings. His stance was so unpopular, in fact, that King Noah sent his soldiers after Alma with orders to murder him (Mosiah 17:3). Alma gave up his position as a priest, which would have been one of the most prominent positions in their society, to challenge the king and live in hiding for what was probably years (Mosiah 17:4). At times, he likely felt lonely and sad. Regardless, he most certainly didn't know that he would become one of the most well-known prophets of our latter-day era. And yet, despite all of this, Alma chose to love the Lord first. He chose to surrender all his earthly prominence to stand for what he knew was right. Despite his uncomely beginning, Alma persisted through his trial of faith and eventually baptized hundreds of Nephites (Mosiah 18:16). Whether as a missionary or member, we too must never allow the praise of men to trespass upon our love for the Lord.

DAKOTA

Elder Gonne and I had never served together as companions, but we always seemed to click. Having met in the MTC, we quickly connected over several similar interests. We often chatted at zone conferences, and I had really come to value him as a friend.

One day, the mission president confided in me that Elder Gonne was struggling. Elder Gonne wasn't excited about the missionary opportunities in his area and was in a slump. So, when the mission president assigned me to be his companion for just one day, I was ecstatic. I thought it would be fun to finally be companions with my friend, and, I hoped, get him excited about missionary work again.

The day started out fine, but it was soon evident that he wasn't enjoying himself. As we went along, I would stop and talk to people along the side of the road, offering them a pamphlet or a pass-along card, while Elder Gonne just stood there in silence next to me. This happened many times. It was awkward. Part of me wanted to stop talking to people, because I could sense his distaste toward me growing each time I did. At least once, I asked him if something was wrong, but he just shook his head. I knew talking with strangers about the gospel was the right thing to do (see *Preach My Gospel*, 161), but I feared that it was somehow going to ruin our friendship. I really didn't want that.

At the end of our day, we discussed what we learned from each other. Elder Gonne didn't have much to say but asked me if there was anything he could do to improve. In that moment, my mind was racing. Should I tell him, "Nothing! You are doing great!" or do I tell him the truth? I knew by telling him the truth, there was a chance I might lose our friendship. I could sense his growing distaste toward me, and this could be the last straw. In that moment, I felt prompted to be honest in the nicest way I could. I first told him all the good things I learned from him that day and then suggested that he engage with more strangers to and from his teaching appointments. I promised blessings, joy, and success if he did so.

Despite my best efforts to be what I thought was as polite and positive as possible, all I got was silence in return. Elder Gonne stared at me from across the table. I don't remember exactly what words he finally used to respond, but in essence, he basically told me, "No. Elder Pierce, you're wrong."

The rest of the night was awkward, and the following morning I packed my bags and headed back to my own area, feeling disheartened.

The whole next week I stressed. What had I done? I thought I had done what the Lord wanted me to do. I had tried to be nice, yet honest. I felt sad. I felt lonely. I had lost my friend.

A week later, I finally got a call from Elder Gonne. I picked up the phone, expecting to get a scolding, but instead heard a roar of "Elder Pierce!"

"Elder Gonne! How's it going?" I asked uncertainly.

"You won't believe what happened this week!" he practically yelled. He then proceeded to tell me miracle after miracle, many of which stemmed from talking to strangers to and from his teaching appointments, and the rest from his positive attitude gained from talking to those same miracle strangers.

For months after that, I would randomly get calls from Elder Gonne and listen to him as he shared all the wonderful miracles happening in his area. Elder Gonne became one of the most successful missionaries in our mission and inspired other missionaries. Today, Elder Gonne and I remain better friends than ever.

This story isn't here to say that you should always be forthcoming with improvements others need to make in their lives. In fact, there may be many situations where you feel prompted to hold back advice. Rather, the point is, like Alma leaving King Noah and all his prominence, we always need to be willing to put our love for the Lord above the praise of men. Just because you don't receive a standing ovation from everyone watching doesn't mean God isn't clapping.

Dakota, left, with Elder Gonne, right, in East Malaysia

2. UNDERSTAND YOUR COMPANION

The next step after loving the Lord is learning to love your neighbor. In a missionary setting, we have often found that this begins with striving to understand your companion. One of the best ways to understand your companion is to listen to them.

21

"When you listen carefully to others, you understand them better. When they know that their thoughts and feelings are important to you, they are more likely to be receptive to your [suggestions], share personal experiences and make [changes]" (*Preach My Gospel*, 187).

DAKOTA

I remember being assigned to be Elder Grey's companion. Elder Grey was new to the mission field, but it was immediately obvious that he was ready to give his "heart, might, mind, and strength" to the work (see D&C 4:2). The first week he worked super hard, got up on time, arrived early for studies, and was memorizing scriptures in Chinese left and right. I was shocked. His "greenie-fire" was real.

By the next week, however, Elder Grey had lost his "greenie-fire." He wasn't waking up on time and sometimes refused to leave the house. He had practically given up on learning Chinese.

Day after day, I tried to encourage him. I invited him to try my exciting new workout routines, shared new Chinese phrases with him I was learning, and attempted to bestow my gospel insights on him. My encouragement, however, only seemed to make him more negative. I was feeling like an absolute failure as a companion and didn't understand what more I could do.

Finally, one day, after cursing at me for trying to get him out of bed, he broke down crying. I remember just sitting there next to him on the bed, praying, pleading with Heavenly Father that he would open up to me. In all honesty, I had no idea why he was crying.

This time, instead of suggesting some magic remedy, I just sat there in silence, waiting. I wasn't sure if he would open up to me, but I realized then that perhaps the best thing I could do was just listen.

After several minutes, he finally broke the dead silence. He began to tell me how much he hated the Church and his mission. He didn't believe in the Book of Mormon and he thought it was all a fraud. He told me the only reason he went on a mission was that he didn't want to let his parents down but that obligation was fading fast. He wanted out.

Realizing that I had only seen the tip of the iceberg, I listened for what I could do to help. We began to read the scriptures out loud together for studies. Then, we worked through some of his doctrinal questions that he had written out. As we discussed his questions and doubts, I often found myself just listening to him. Elder Grey was well-read and knew his gospel doctrine. However, even as I sat there listening, it was clear that his demeanor was changing for the better. Even though we weren't able to answer all of his questions, Elder Grey gradually decided to stay on his mission.

Looking back, I wish I had listened to Elder Grey sooner. I was overly confident in my suggestions for exercise, language study, and gospel insights. I believed they were the answers to Elder Grey's problems—problems that I didn't even take the time to understand. I quickly learned that "the interpersonal efforts that inevitably succeed are those in which the messenger stops dictating and starts discovering what the recipient wants" (Dale Carnegie, *How to Win Friends and Influence People in the Digital Age*, 31). "More important than speaking is listening. . . . If we listen with love, we won't need to wonder what to say. It will be given to us—by the Spirit and by our friends" (Jeffrey R. Holland, "Witnesses unto Me," *Ensign*, May 2001, 15). Striving to understand others can take great humility and patience, but it will inspire the best in those around you.

Elder Grey, left, and Dakota, right, in East Malaysia

3. JUST SERVE

Even though listening is essential to any relationship, overanalyzing a companion's motives or situation can, in some instances, be detrimental. Sometimes the answer lies not in dissecting the past, but in forging the future. In our missionary work, we called this just serving.

As an extreme example, think of the Anti-Nephi-Lehies. No amount of preaching or smooth-talking would have ever converted the wicked Lamanites. It was only by experiencing the faithfulness of the Anti-Nephi-Lehies as they "prostrated themselves . . . and began to call on the name of the Lord . . . prais[ing] God even in the very act of perishing under the sword" that their hearts were softened (Alma 24:21–23). No one is asking you to risk your life to soften your companion's heart, but serving righteously with all your might can uplift the deflated, soften the rebellious, and cure dissatisfaction—feelings that we all endure.

MATTHEW

"What in the world! What has been going on in this area?" I asked myself. I had arrived in my new area only to realize that my new companion, Elder Henderson, had essentially no people to teach, no one coming to church, and wasn't sure who or where most of the less active members lived. *What are we supposed to do all day?* I thought. I was tempted to ask Elder Hendersen what he had been doing all this time but knew that wouldn't do any good. I could tell Elder Hendersen was stressed. The best thing to do, I realized, was exactly that: just do.

"So, who can we visit today?" I asked. Together, we searched through past teaching records and went over the list of branch members. We wrote down the names of less active members we didn't know and immediately set up a meeting with the branch leadership to learn more about the members. Without thinking too much about the area's past, Elder Henderson and I launched into the work.

The weeks flew by. Elder Henderson and I were working incredibly hard and we were having so much fun. Miracles were happening daily. We had the Spirit. We were working with active and less active members, inviting them to teach with us, and inviting everyone we saw, it seemed, to come unto Christ.

One night Elder Henderson approached me. "Elder Spurrier, I have to be honest with you. That first night we were together, I felt so awkward because we literally had no work in our area. My previous companion had struggled to be obedient and work hard and it had really taken a toll on me. I was worn out and felt out of place. Then you showed up and started talking about people we could baptize, less active members we could visit, and how to plan well. I just thought you were crazy! But I decided, why not? Since then, I have had so much fun doing missionary work, and we have helped so many people. I'm loving this."

In hindsight, I could have chosen to first focus on why there was no work going on in the area. I could have made Elder Henderson feel bad for everything he had not been doing. But by not doing so, perhaps I had given Elder Henderson a free restart. By simply serving as hard as I could, miracles followed, and Elder Henderson was all in.

Elder Henderson became one of the hardest working companions I've ever served with. He later told me that my example of service "changed the course of his mission and life." Subsequently, Elder Henderson went on to change the lives of many missionaries he served with. To this day, we remain close friends.

Matthew, left, and Elder Henderson, right, in Malaysia

Don't feel like you always need to know the backstory to every situation. Often the best remedy for helping your companion is just doing what is right and assuming the best in others. Many missionaries are eager to work hard, feel successful, and help God's children. Sometimes, it just takes someone on our team that can give us a kick-start. You can be that spark.

"One of the greatest secrets of missionary work is work! If a missionary works, he will get the Spirit . . . and he will be happy. There will be no homesickness, no worrying about families, for all time and talents and interests are centered on the work of the ministry. Work, work, work—there is no satisfactory substitute, especially in missionary work" (Ezra Taft Benson, *The Teachings of Ezra Taft Benson*, 200).

4. USE COMMON SENSE AND COMPROMISE

MATTHEW

"Welcome to your new area!" I said to Elder Carlson. Earlier in my mission, I had lived in the same apartment as Elder Carlson, but now we were going to be companions. I was excited. Elder Carlson was known as an excellent teacher with legendary language skills. However, I was also nervous, because when we had lived together before, he wasn't the most obedient missionary. Although I wanted to follow the rules, I didn't want to make things awkward between us if we disagreed on what we should and shouldn't be doing.

For the first few weeks, things were mostly positive. We were working hard, and I was learning so much from Elder Carlson. For instance, every day he would generously take fifteen minutes of his precious language study time to teach me hundreds of new Malay words. However, we always seemed to disagree on two things. First, I didn't think he should take an hour nap every day after lunch, and second, he thought we shouldn't proselyte in the rain (it rained every day). We continually argued on these subjects, and for weeks, they were areas of contention.

Finally, one day, I had an idea. "Elder Carlson," I said, "how about you take just a thirty-minute nap before we go out each day, and then no matter if it's raining, pouring, or the old man is snoring, we will go out and talk with people about the gospel, even if we don't have something concretely planned to do."

Elder Carlson thought about it and then agreed.

The compromise worked. Most days, Elder Carlson continued to take a thirty-minute nap while I confirmed our teaching appointments or called previous contacts. As the weeks went on, Elder Carlson began to enjoy getting out of the house no matter the conditions. We saw more and more miracles as we put our trust in the Lord and used His time more effectively.

The last day we were together, Elder Carlson said to me, "Elder Spurrier, thank you. This was the hardest I've ever worked on my mission. I have no regrets. We've seen miracles, and I know we've done the Lord's work."

Elder Carlson had worked harder in those weeks than ever before, and, although he still took a nap every day, through compromise, he was willing to follow many of the other rules he previously hadn't. In fact, by giving him thirty minutes to nap every day, we were able to help many more of God's children because we were then able to get out of our house more and had less contention.

The bottom line is that you are beholden to your mission companion only insofar as practical rules dictate, but aren't you really there to be accountable to God? So, if something doesn't feel right, use your brain and speak up.

Now, as a word of warning, some things are probably okay to compromise on, and other rules should never be compromised. As you consider how to help your companionship and work through misunderstandings or differences in opinions, remember that you can always talk with your missionary leaders or mission president for advice. Common sense and compromise can often be seen clearer from an outside perspective. When it comes to heated disagreements, it can be easy to lose sight of the forest in the trees. Responsible outside sources can help.

OBEDIENCE BRINGS BLESSINGS

Stephen Covey taught to always "keep the main thing the main thing" (*First Things First*, Stephen R. Covey, 75). In this case, the main thing is Christ, not the rules. Keeping rules for the sake of rules will never work in the long-term. Your *why* must be much deeper than that. Your *why* must be rooted in Christ.

As Boyd K. Packer taught, "True doctrine, understood, changes attitudes and behavior. The study of the doctrine of the gospel will improve behavior quicker than a study of behavior will improve behavior" (*Preach My Gospel*, 19). Or as Alma put it, "Yea, [the word of God] had had more powerful effect upon the minds of the people than the sword, [the rules], or anything else" (Alma 31:5).

Obedience should stem from your love for God and your appreciation for Christ's Atonement, not from your idealization of the exactly obedient missionary or perfect human being.

Missionaries must first understand that the missionary rules "availeth nothing except it were through the atonement of [Christ's] blood" (Mosiah 3:15). Your priority is first to Christ and then to the rules and commandments, never the other way around.

As you do the Lord's work, you will want and need His help. Doing the Lord's work His way will allow the Spirit to be with you more abundantly. "As you try to follow His commandments [and mission standards], He will bless you to know what to say and do" (Elder Erich W. Kopischke, "Courage to Live the Gospel," *Friend*, March 2009). We promise you that missionary work is a lot more rewarding and fun when you have the Lord helping you. Consistent obedience is the first step in maintaining the Lord's help and showing you have faith in Jesus Christ.

There will be many times when you might not understand why a specific rule exists. If you find yourself asking why, follow the example of Adam: When an angel appeared to Adam and asked him, "Why dost thou offer sacrifices unto the Lord?" Adam replied, "I know not, save the Lord commanded me" (Moses 5:6). Adam was blessed with prosperity because he followed the Lord's command without a perfect knowledge. Sometimes, we must trust Heavenly Father and Jesus Christ's commandments without knowing exactly why.

Along this same line, Ether taught, "Ye receive no witness until after the trial of your faith" (Ether 12:6). We are not telling you to blindly follow everything you're told to do, but rather asking you to choose to have faith. You can and should ask questions. "If you have questions about a standard, prayerfully ask the Lord to help you understand its importance, and then if needed, ask your companion, your young missionary leaders, or either of your mission leaders for help" (*Missionary Standards*, "Message from the First Presidency and Quorum of the Twelve Apostles," 3). As you are obedient, you will see miracles unfold in front of you. Be open to how and when the Lord will bless you, but know He most certainly will.

Jesus taught, "If any man will do [the Father's] will [by following a commandment or standard], he shall know of the doctrine, whether it be of God, or whether I speak of myself" (John 7:17). We testify that Jesus meant what He said.

CHALLENGE #2

THINK ABOUT A COMMANDMENT OR GUIDELINE YOU STRUGGLE WITH NOW (AS A MEMBER) AND MAKE PLANS TO CHANGE. JOURNAL THE BLESSINGS YOU SEE.

HELPFUL SUGGESTIONS

- Ask family and friends how obedience on their missions has blessed them.
- Read *Missionary Standards for Disciples of Jesus Christ.*

CHAPTER 3
LIVING WITH SOMEONE 24/7

⎯⎯⎯⎯⎯ ❦ ⎯⎯⎯⎯⎯

As you saw in the survey in the introduction, a majority of returned missionaries, when asked what the most difficult obstacle of their mission was, responded with one word—companions. We can vouch that living with someone 24/7 requires sincere efforts to be humble, courageous, and patient. The good news is these efforts will transform you into a more Christlike missionary and human being.

Companions have taught us so much about ourselves, some of these lessons being what's important to us, our pet peeves, and how we handle various situations. These priceless life lessons, although perhaps challenging in the moment, will teach you how to live and work through interpersonal conflicts with roommates, coworkers, and a future spouse.

SOMETIMES COMPANIONSHIPS ARE JUST HARD—THAT IS NORMAL

MATTHEW

My six weeks in the MTC were undoubtedly some of the hardest six weeks of my entire mission. I arrived at the MTC wide-eyed and excited to meet my first companion, Elder Wicker. For the next six weeks, we struggled together to learn how to be missionaries and speak Malay. As it turned out, Elder Wicker and I were very different. He was homeschooled; I went to public school. He wanted to speak Chinese; I wanted to speak Malay. He liked singing in the choir; I enjoyed playing sports. The list could go on forever. However, despite our differences in personality, upbringing, and seemingly everything else, I hoped our companionship would run smoothly.

It didn't. Just three days in, Elder Wicker and I hit our first bump.

"I'm excited to become friends," I said to Elder Wicker.

"We are not friends, Elder Spurrier. We are just companions," he replied.

Our entire district overheard the exchange, and awkwardness filled the room. However, I was determined to work things out. After a first week full of contention, I thought giving him a gift might help, so I got him and the rest of our district new ties.

"Elder Wicker, I got you a tie," I said one night. Grinning, I held it out to him.

"No thank you," he said.

Ouch.

Matthew's MTC district all wearing the matching ties except for his companion, Elder Wicker

As the weeks passed, everything I did seemed to annoy him, and everything he did seemed to annoy me. Maybe it was the new style of missionary life, or maybe we were just too different, but I began counting down the days to when our companionship would end. I remember writing home and asking my parents, "What is wrong with me? I've always gotten along well with people, but we just can't figure it out!" We couldn't agree on what to teach or what to do with our exercise time. We struggled to stay within sight and sound of each other and often got into heated arguments. I felt like I was failing as a missionary, and I know Elder Wicker was not happy to be there either. I prayed each day asking God, "What am I supposed to learn from this?"

A few weeks later, things started to get better. My nightly prayers began to fill my heart with more empathy and patience, and I worked hard at trying not to do the things that bothered Elder Wicker. By working individually to unify ourselves with the Spirit, Elder Wicker and I found ourselves finally beginning to become unified. We started agreeing on more decisions, teaching better lessons, and finding genuine interest in each other's families, pre-mission lives, and hobbies. By our final week together, Elder Wicker and I were no longer arguing, and I could say we were friends.

A month after the MTC, Elder Wicker emailed me, and we apologized to each other. Later, both his and my mission leaders told me that he was dealing with other personal things in the MTC that had, in turn, affected our relationship. Although Elder Wicker and I never became best friends, we moved past our differences and had good conversations. There were just some things going on in Elder Wicker's life at the time that were outside my understanding and control.

Remember, patience doesn't just mean waiting. It also means being proactive in controlling what you can control. When I focused on unifying myself with the Spirit, things weren't perfect, but we got along despite our individual problems. Patience involves understanding that few solutions are instantaneous, but "by [consistent] small and simple things are great things brought to pass" (Alma 37:6).

Sometimes, all you need to do is your best with a companion and ask yourself, "What can I learn from this experience? How can I serve my companion? And how can we still accomplish the Lord's work?"

God commanded us to "go forth in the power of [His] Spirit, preaching [His] gospel, two by two" (D&C 42:6). However, He never said that it would be easy. Going "forth in the power of [His] Spirit" means first unifying yourself with the Spirit and then your companionship. This process can be difficult, but it's so worth it.

DON'T BURY PROBLEMS, TALK THEM OUT

DAKOTA

I had been with Elder Yor for six weeks when we started to have problems. Until then, we had been doing great: the area was on fire, we had people on date for baptism, and Elder Yor was teaching me how to cook!

Dakota learning from Elder Yor how to cook enchiladas from scratch

Then, for no apparent reason, our companionship unity fell apart. We couldn't agree on daily plans, who to focus our teaching on, what to teach, or even who to talk with in the street. We couldn't have been more out of sync. Things got to a point where we couldn't even pray together without arguing about who would say the prayer.

A wise teacher once taught me to talk with my companions about companionship conflicts sooner rather than later. Otherwise, the tension would continue to build and then explode all at once.

So that's what I did. When I could feel the Spirit being driven away by the contention between us, I would stop whatever we were doing, ask if there was anything I was doing that was bothering him and what I could do to improve—before launching into my side of the story. This helped a lot, at least temporarily. By the end of our talks, we would hug it out and tell each other we were sorry and how much we appreciated each other. Nevertheless, no matter how many times we talked things over, nothing permanently changed. We would set specific goals to do things differently, and it would get better for a few days. But by the end of the week, we would be arguing again, and I would come home at night wanting to scream at him.

It wasn't that Elder Yor was a bad guy. In fact, he seemed like a great dude. He was a farmer from Idaho and was on his mission for the right reasons. But no matter what we tried, we just didn't get along. Talking things out had always permanently helped in other companionships. Why not this time? Truthfully, I felt he was maybe hiding something else. Was there perhaps something personal he was dealing with? Otherwise, why couldn't we get along? Was I the problem? We had tried everything and yet nothing had worked. We, two fully committed missionaries, weren't getting along—at all. I didn't get it.

Finally one day, Elder Yor came to me and said, "Elder Pierce, I need to tell you something."

Curious, I nodded, encouraging him to go ahead.

"Well, you see, I've been a bit distracted by Sister Coles lately. I've come to really like her."

Wide-eyed, my jaw dropped. "Wait, you mean the same Sister Coles that's in our district? The one that we see almost every day?"

"Yep," he said. "I don't want to jump the gun, but I think I want to marry her."

I just about fell out of my chair in shock. My companion had fallen in love with a sister in our district. Looking back, it was no wonder that he and I had been having problems. On top of our missionary responsibilities, he'd been balancing the priority of his future wife.

Finally understanding his distraction, our talks became much more effective. Although things were never perfect, I now understood what was on his mind, and we were able to work through it. Although you probably won't fall in love with a sister or elder while on your mission (and I hope you don't!), you will certainly be tempted to hold on to other issues. While it's good to swallow small, unimportant things that bother you, when you start trying to bury issues that continue to weigh on you, things tend to backfire. In the moment, burying your problems can seem like the right thing to do, but generally it's not. When larger issues are buried, pain, jealousy, and hatred grow, and the Spirit often disappears. Jesus taught, "The spirit of contention is not of me, but is of the devil" (3 Nephi 11:29).

On the other hand, not burying your issues doesn't mean you need to rage on your companion's every little mistake. Bring things up that continue to bother you, but be flexible and, most important, be nice. This isn't a contest to see who can come up with the longest list of criticisms or conflicts. Ask what you can do to improve first before you start shoving over theories about your companion's fundamental character flaws. Then suggest some potential specific solutions that include your participation. Being honest, flexible, and proactive within your companionships is underrated and solves most problems before they can begin.

In the end, things worked out for Elder Yor and Sister Coles. Both served honorable missions, and when they returned home, they ended up getting married. Now they have two kids. Through it all, Elder Yor and I have stayed good friends.

Dakota, left, and Elder Yor, right

THE COWBOY WHO WOULDN'T STOP TALKING

DAKOTA

Elder Free and I still talk on the phone weekly. I consider him one of my best friends. Nevertheless, things weren't always this smooth. With his hard accent and cowboy boots, I thought he was preparing for a rodeo when he first showed up at the MTC. But there he was, Elder Free, my first companion.

Elder Free and Dakota during one of their first days at the MTC

Socially, Elder Free and I were very different. Elder Free loved to talk, and I quickly realized that I did not. Elder Free would strike up conversations with seemingly every person we walked past. It took us forever to get anywhere, because Elder Free was always busy talking with someone. I about lost my mind. I quickly learned that if this companionship was going to be successful, I needed to not only tolerate Elder Free but also embrace him.

A couple of weeks later, I had learned how to "yeeeeehaw" every different kind of "yeeeeehaw" imaginable, and I thought I might change my career from an MIT rocket scientist to a next-generation cowboy. Fortunately, Elder Free and I became good friends by embracing our differences. However, in spite of our newfound friendship, we struggled to keep some of the basic rules, especially being "able to see and hear your companion at all times" (*Missionary Standards*, 2.2.2). Elder Free chatted with everyone, and sometimes I just didn't pay attention. Other times (as you can see in the following photo), Elder Free was just a bit different.

Elder Free climbing a fifty-foot tree at the MTC

One day, our district leader sat us down. "Look, Elders," he said. "Obviously you're struggling to stay within sight and sound of each other. Elder Pierce, give me your handbag."

Cautiously, I handed over my handbag, unsure about what he was going to do.

He unclipped the shoulder strap and shortened it. Then, clipping one side to Elder Free's right hip belt loop and the other to my left hip belt loop, he sighed and said, "We're gonna have you try something else. For the next ten hours, you two will stay clipped together no matter what. This way you won't be tempted to leave each other."

Elder Free and Dakota clipped together at the MTC

Following his guidance, we went to class, ate meals, taught lessons, and talked with everyone—tied together. I had no choice but to stand there next to him as he chit-chatted on and on. It killed me. Nevertheless, we quickly became known at the MTC as the cowboy and the nerd who couldn't stay together so they had to be tied together. Rest assured, we learned our lesson.

Nine MTC weeks later, we parted ways, and I was glad to be off on a new adventure. I figured my stint as a social cowboy was complete. Five months later, however, I got the news that I had been assigned to serve with Elder Free again.

That day was full of mixed emotions. Part of me was stoked to be with an old friend again, but another part of me didn't know if I could handle embracing his social cowboy way of life for another six weeks (six weeks equals one transfer). What I didn't know was that it was going to be much longer.

At first, things went better than I thought. We spent six weeks working hard and having fun. Then we had another six weeks. Three months later, I was secretly excited to move on. Transfers were coming up, and I knew I had to be transferred.

Our mission president never left anyone together longer than three months, and we had already been in the MTC together.

Transfer day arrived. I looked for my name across the computer screen, scanning all the different zones. Unable to find my name, I finally opened the page for our current zone. There we were. Elder Free and I, companions for yet another six weeks. I couldn't believe it.

It wasn't that he was disobedient or lazy. To be honest, in some aspects Elder Free was more hard working and obedient than I was. He definitely talked with more people about the gospel than I did. Rather, I just needed a change of scenery. I had been embracing the same person's differences for almost six months.

That was the low point of my mission. I was teaching people that they have a Heavenly Father who knew them by name, but did I really believe that? Did God really care about me? If so, how could He stick me with the same social cowboy companion again, and again, and again? Had I just been forgotten on the transfer board?

I half-expected the mission president to call and tell me why he had left me with Elder Free again, but the call never came. I thought maybe God would send down some sign to let me know that yes, I was in the right place at the right time, but the sign never came. Despite the lack of divine intervention, I got through those next few days and weeks. Things turned out okay, but it was nothing better than an average transfer. No stand-out miracles, and, sadly, no calls from the mission president. But, hey, we sure talked to a lot of people.

Six weeks later, transfer news came, and we were finally separated.

A year later, I was serving with a different companion. One day he asked me, "Elder Pierce, how did you learn to talk with so many people?"

Taken aback, I thought about it. I had always been an introvert. What was this guy talking about?

"No really," he said. "It's like the more people you talk to, the more energy you get. How do you do that?"

Then it hit me. Elder Free. It was only then that I realized that God *had* cared. No, the mission president hadn't forgotten about me for all those transfers. No, my twenty-seven weeks as a social cowboy hadn't been a mistake. The entire time I'd been becoming social and I hadn't even realized it.

WHERE'S MY PERFECT COMPANION?

DAKOTA

One day during district meeting, our district leader handed out a piece of paper listing thirty-two attributes, including humble, intelligent, friendly, and honest.

He asked us to be honest with ourselves and write a score (one to ten) on how well we thought we embodied each attribute, ten being like Jesus Christ. Wanting to be fair, I gave myself a few threes, a good number of fives, and a rare seven or eight.

After we had finished, he handed us a second piece of paper, with the same attributes listed again. He then asked us to write down a score (one to ten) for what we wanted in a companion. I began to score my ideal companion and realized that I was only writing down nines and tens.

I then compared who I was to what I was looking for. It was lopsided. To say the least, I would have been disappointed to be assigned myself as a companion. I was not the kind of person I expected others to be, which is otherwise known as *hypocrisy*.

ME:	MY IDEAL COMPANION:
8 Intelligent	10 Intelligent
2 Thoughtful	10 Thoughtful
3 Cheerful	8 Cheerful
4 Compassionate	10 Compassionate
9 Humble	10 Humble
7 Kind	10 Kind
5 People-Oriented	10 People-Oriented
9 Work-Oriented	10 Work-Oriented
4 Affectionate	10 Affectionate
9 Confident	7 Confident
3 Curteous	10 Curteous
7 Disciplined	10 Disciplined
6 Spiritual	10 Spiritual
5 Friendly	10 Friendly
1 Reliable	10 Reliable
3 Considerate	10 Considerate
8 Long-term Oriented	10 Long-term Oriented
3 Short-term Oriented	6 Short-term Oriented
8 Honest	10 Honest
2 Patient	10 Patient
5 Prudent	10 Prudent
8 Forgiving	10 Forgiving
7 Idealistic	10 Idealistic
9 Articulate	10 Articulate
7 Thrifty	9 Thrifty
9 Chaste	10 Chaste
7 Trustworthy	10 Trustworthy
6 Loyal	10 Loyal
4 Helpful	9 Helpful
8 Obedient	10 Obedient
4 Courageous	10 Courageous
6 Realistic	10 Realistic

Dakota's original, lopsided attribute scorecard

It wasn't just me. The other missionaries around me were having the same issues as they compared their scores. Since then, I've realized that in healthy companionships, missionaries focus on each other's strengths while considering their own shortcomings. Jesus taught us,

> And why beholdest thou the mote that is in thy brother's eye, but considerest not the beam that is in thine own eye?
>
> Thou hypocrite, first cast out the beam out of thine own eye; and then shalt thou see clearly to cast out the mote out of thy brother's eye. (Matthew 7:3, 5)

We believe Jesus Christ was perfect, and He is. However, if Jesus were here with us now, would we question His perfections? Might we find fault in His actions?

Joseph Smith once asked a congregation, "Do you think that even Jesus, if He were here, would be without fault in *your* eyes?" (*Teachings of Presidents of the Church: Joseph Smith*, 522; emphasis added). Might it be our pride that gets in the way?

C. S. Lewis said this about pride:

> Pride gets no pleasure out of having something, only out of having more of it than the next man. We say that people are proud of being rich, or clever, or good-looking, but they are not, they are proud of being richer, cleverer, or better-looking than others. If everyone else became equally rich, or clever, or good-looking there would be nothing to be proud about. It is the comparison that makes you proud: The pleasure of being above the rest. Once the element of competition has gone, pride has gone *(Mere Christianity*, 95).

God's plan is not a race that only a certain amount of people can win. It's not a class in which only so many A grades can be handed out, or a university with only so many open spots for the most accomplished students. His class is not graded on a curve (see Matthew 20:1–16; 1 Nephi 22:28). That's why learning from others while loving them, rather than judging them or competing with them, is essential to becoming like Christ.

That being said, learning from and loving others doesn't mean we should embrace everything about a person or shrug off every wrongdoing as no big deal. The pure love of Christ takes many forms outside of the traditional definition of love, including setting boundaries and, more important, keeping them.

Christ taught us to forgive and love all people. He made a point to become friends with sinners. "However, Jesus had boundaries. When [the people of]

Nazareth tried to kill Him, He never returned (see Luke 4:29–30). He told Peter when he had crossed a line (see Matthew 16:22–23). He called out leaders for hypocrisy" (Hank R. Smith, Twitter; see Matthew 23). He kicked businessmen and women out of the temple (see Matthew 21:12–13). "Clear boundaries are Christlike" (Smith, Twitter).

Your boundaries will likely create *conflict*, but nowhere in the scriptures does the Lord warn against *conflict*. "He only warns against *contention*" (Ryan Morgenegg and Kevin P. Miller, *Three Ways to Keep Conflict from Becoming Contention*, emphasis added; see Mosiah 18:21). In fact, conflict can be viewed as a growth opportunity. The strength of a relationship often depends on differences, not similarities (Morgenegg and Miller, *Three Ways*). Contention begins when conflict becomes personal. We must learn to separate the sin from the sinner.

Forget the notion of a perfect companion. Remember to embrace the differences within your companionships, learn from conflicts while steering clear of contention, and protect your boundaries.

SOME COMPANIONSHIPS ARE JUST NATURAL

There is no better feeling than getting along naturally with your companion. It will happen, and it's the BEST! You might have a ton of similarities, but you also might have strengths that complement each other's weaknesses.

MATTHEW

I remember meeting Elder Yakob on our first day as companions. We couldn't have been more different. He loved computer science, wore glasses, and was quiet. I, on the other hand, loved playing sports, always cracked jokes, and talked loudly. As Elder Yakob and I began to discuss our area, two simple things quickly united us: our love for missionary work and willingness to work hard and learn from each other. Elder Yakob and I began sharing with each other the best practices and missionary methods we had learned from previous companionships. I shared how to powerfully teach short lessons and how to talk with everyone. Elder Yakob taught me how to effectively prioritize planning each day and have daily contact with the people we taught. As time went on, I found myself enjoying learning random nerdy facts from him and creating our own inside jokes. Eventually I realized that we had cultivated an unusually amazing friendship. We enjoyed listening to church music together, making mac and cheese for lunch, and sweating our guts out as we biked for miles on end. Although on the surface we were very different, we both had the same desire. Both of us wanted to serve the Lord with all our "heart, might, mind, and strength" and leave our area better than we found it (see D&C 4:2). This was the only similarity we needed. It bonded us together as real friends and united companions as we progressed in the work of the Lord.

Today, we remain great friends and continue to learn from each other.

Elder Yakob, left, and Matthew, right

If [men and women] humble themselves before me, and have faith in me, then will I make weak [and different] things become strong unto them. (Ether 12:27)

God has taught us that if we come unto Him, He will show us our weaknesses, but the recognition of those weaknesses often takes root in our differences. Companions are great for pushing you out of your comfort zone. If you're willing, any companion will show you things about yourself that you either didn't know existed or were too scared to face.

MATTHEW

Elder Abel would be my final companion. For my last three months as a missionary, I wanted to "leave it all on the table."

While waiting for the subway one day, Elder Abel turned to me and said, "Let's sing a hymn to that guy over there to help him feel the Spirit."

Ahhhh! I thought. I hated singing for people, but Elder Abel didn't know that. He knew I had been in a band and played guitar and piano, so he naturally wanted to sing with me. Frightened, I walked over with Elder Abel and began to sing "Nearer, My God to Thee" to this random guy. It was a huge success. More than once we used this tactic, and more than once people ended up crying because of the Spirit they felt. Elder Abel and I always pushed each other to be better, and he helped me see talents in myself that I previously saw as weaknesses. Today, I love singing for people—for my family, my wife, and sometimes still complete strangers.

Let your companions push you and take you outside your comfort zone. Do the same for them. As you do this, you will be fulfilling scripture, and your "weak things [will] become strong" (Ether 12:27).

MATTHEW AND DAKOTA

Oddly enough, I messaged Dakota (future Elder Pierce) on Facebook three months before we entered the MTC after I saw him post about his call to the Singapore mission. We briefly met in the MTC, and I sat next to him on the plane to Singapore, where we contacted our first stranger together. Over a year later, as rare as it was, Dakota, a Chinese-speaking elder and myself, a Malay-speaking elder, were assigned as companions.

Despite having different assigned mission languages, Dakota and I not only got along, but we quickly became best friends. Missionary work had never been easier, and I always knew he had my back. We would stop cars in transit to share the gospel, pray with people in the streets, exchange crazy mission stories, create fun trainings and lessons, and talk to everyone possible about Jesus Christ. We quickly learned what the other was good at and leveraged our individual strengths to unitedly find, teach, baptize, retain, and reactivate God's children. Things went so well that the mission president kept us together for almost five months, and our relationship blossomed.

Today, Dakota and I are still best friends. Although we attended college on opposite sides of the country, we still see each other when we can and talk almost every day. He was one of my groomsmen, and we even decided to write this book together. We keep each other in check, continue to push each other outside our comfort zones, and are planning on one day being neighbors. Certain people you meet on your mission will become lifelong friends, and working with them to progress God's work will create moments of life you will cherish forever.

Matthew, left, with Dakota, right, as one of Matthew's groomsmen

Chances are, you will get a whole array of companions—some you initially like, some you don't; some who are very different from you, and some who will become lifelong friends. That's normal.

Mission presidents often get two types of phone calls or emails: First, "President, my companion and I are struggling for such-and-such a reason. We are working on it but just wanted to let you know." Second, "President, my companion is struggling for such-and-such a reason. Can you do something about it?" Be the first type! Don't be a tattletale. Be a force for good! Love your companion unconditionally, and never give up on them. Regardless of the challenges, living with someone 24/7 gives you the opportunity to grow personally and learn from others. Enjoy the process.

CHALLENGE #3

BE A FRIEND TO ONE PERSON WHO DOESN'T HAVE MANY FRIENDS.

HELPFUL SUGGESTIONS

- Ask family and friends about what they did on their missions to work with all types of companions.

- Practice putting others' needs before your own by serving those around you: iron someone's shirt, clean the dishes, offer someone a ride home, etc. Be creative!

- "If you cannot give when you have little, you will not be likely to give when you have everything" (J. Michael Pinegar, "The Lord's Goods"). Even if you aren't rich yet, this doesn't mean you can't give now: pay your tithing in full, donate a monthly fast offering, give your time to a homeless shelter or nursing home, ask your parents "What can I do to help around the house?," etc.

- Take the attribute test: use the picture above with the attributes listed to grade yourself. Pick a couple attributes you'd like to work on.

- Go through a "companionship inventory" with siblings, parents or friends (*Preach My Gospel*, 154). Tell them what you admire about them, share with them your goals and ask how you can improve.

CHAPTER 4

YOUR PERFECT COMPANION: THE HOLY GHOST

In chapter three, we told you to forget the notion of a "perfect companion." Now, we are going to ask you to remember it, because, outside of not having a physical body, the constant companionship of the Holy Ghost is your perfect companion. We don't typically speak of the Holy Ghost as being perfect, especially since He still lacks a physical body, but indeed, "the Holy Ghost works in *perfect* unity with Heavenly Father and Jesus Christ" (*True to the Faith*, 82; emphasis added). He *could* also work in perfect unity with us, but because we as humans are far from perfect, we often get along better with our imperfect physical companions than with Him. So next time you start wishing you had a perfect companion, remember that you already do, and ask yourself, "How well are the Holy Ghost and I getting along?"

Jesus asks us to "be perfect even as [He] . . . is perfect" (3 Nephi 12:48). It's a bit hard to measure perfection, but one sure way to understand our progress is to recognize when we are becoming more in tune and unified with the Holy Ghost. Since the Holy Ghost is in perfect unity with Christ, if we can become perfectly in tune with the Holy Ghost, then we can eventually become perfect, just as Christ has asked us to be. (See "Be Ye Therefore Perfect—Eventually," Jeffrey R. Holland, *Ensign*, Nov. 2017.)

Nevertheless, it's safe to say that learning how to recognize and tune into the Holy Ghost's frequency is a lifelong process. In our mid-twenties, we are still in the beginning stages of our journey to learn how to work with Him. Modern-day Apostles and General Authorities have written full-length books and sermons specifically on how to recognize Him. (See *Led by Divine Design*, Ronald A. Rasband, *Ensign*, Nov. 2017; *Guided by the Holy Spirit*, Boyd K. Packer, *Ensign*, May 2011.) Even many of them have admitted that they are still working on recognizing the Spirit themselves. President Henry B. Eyring said, "I work on [recognizing the

Spirit] all the time . . . it is hard" (Face to Face with President Eyring and Elder Holland).

What we're trying to say is that this chapter on the Holy Ghost isn't here to feed you a meal—it's here to make you hungry. We want to inspire you to begin (or try harder on) your journey to recognize the Spirit, not have us complete the journey for you.

Despite the attention to detail and wholehearted effort it takes to recognize the Spirit, we testify that there is NO BETTER FEELING IN THE WORLD than recognizing the Spirit working in your life. It serves as a testament that you are in the right place at the right time and that God really does care.

WAIT . . . I CAN BE A MISSIONARY NOW?

Right now, even before you begin your mission, the Holy Ghost is already your companion. Don't think that the Holy Ghost wants to wait until you have a badge on your chest to help you do missionary work. So, what are you waiting for?

DAKOTA

One of my most memorable missionary experiences happened before I began my mission. I was a freshman at MIT in Boston, just a regular teenaged Church member. Having already read the Book of Mormon and gotten my clear *why* to serve a mission, I had been praying to learn how to follow the Spirit.

One day, as I was biking through the crisp fall air back to my college dorm from stake conference, I passed a homeless lady. At first, I didn't think anything of it. I had passed hundreds of homeless people in Boston that year and never once stopped to talk with any of them. I considered myself introverted and didn't see any real point in talking with them. Besides, I was a poor college student and couldn't afford to give them the money they needed.

However, that day, as I passed the lady on the street, the strongest feeling came over me. It was honestly more than a feeling. It was almost like a voice. It said, "Go ask her if she needs any help." I brushed the thought aside and kept biking. I wanted to get home to my warm dormitory and eat lunch. I was starving.

Before I could bike through the next intersection, the thought came again, only stronger this time. "Go ask her if she needs any help."

I asked myself, "If I go and ask her if she needs any help, what's the worst that could happen?"

Gathering my courage, I turned around and rode back to where she was camped out. I leaned my bike against a tree and walked over to her. She was in a makeshift tent of sorts, and I cautiously called to her, "Hey! Do you need any help?"

She leaned up from her sleeping bag, squinted at me, and then called back, "Are you Mormon?"

Caught off guard, I looked down at my chest, thinking I might be somehow wearing a missionary badge or something. Nope, just my regular old shirt and tie.

"Yes I am!" I said. "How'd you know?"

"I don't know," she said. "Just a lucky guess. I lost my Book of Mormon a while ago and I have been looking for the elders ever since. Do you have an extra copy of the Book of Mormon by chance?"

I practically fell over dead. *Is this what happens every time you talk to homeless people?* I thought. What's more, I usually didn't carry a Book of Mormon, but that morning I had decided to put one in my backpack for some reason.

I handed her my extra copy of the Book of Mormon and watched as she smiled and carefully turned the pages.

Two hours later, I left her where I had found her, having given her my phone number, three dollars, and a paperback copy of the Book of Mormon. I never got a call or saw her again, although when I biked along that street, I often thought of her. Sometimes the experience seems so miraculous that I wonder if she had just been an angel of sorts, put there to answer an eighteen-year-old's prayer about how to follow the Spirit. Some people might call this a coincidence, but I choose to believe that coincidences are just the times God wants to remain anonymous (see Albert Einstein, *The World As I See It*).

The bottom line is that you can be a missionary now. God promises that as you do His work, you will receive "guidance about where to go or what to do" (*Preach My Gospel*, 4); however, these promises aren't predicated on being a full-time missionary. Not having a badge should never get in the way of you following the Holy Ghost or sharing the gospel.

ARE YOU WIZARDS OR SOMETHING?

MATTHEW AND DAKOTA

The week was almost over, and Dakota and I hadn't hit our goal of finding fifteen solid contacts. It was a Sunday night, and the Singapore subway station was bustling with people hurrying to and fro. No one seemed to want to stop and talk with us. They were "too busy." We discussed what we should do with the remaining ten minutes of the day. Should we call more past contacts and see if one of them could meet? Should we sing a song to get people's attention? The only thought that came to our mind was to pray. As we prayed, we basically pleaded, "Heavenly Father, please give us the Spirit, and guide us to the final person we are supposed to meet today." We began walking down a hallway in the subway station, trying to *feel* who we were supposed to talk to.

All of a sudden, we heard, "Elders!" We looked down the hallway and saw a Filipina woman and her friend coming toward us.

"Hello, Sister! Are you a member of the Church?" Dakota asked.

"Yes, Elders," she said, but then for some unknown reason, she sprinted away. Her friend began to run away as well, but we yelled, "Wait!" Although the first woman had already turned the corner, her friend slowly walked back and asked, "Who are you guys?"

We began explaining our purpose and asking her questions about her life. Her name was Sandra, and she worked full time as a housemaid. We explained how we represented Jesus Christ and were there to help her come closer to her Father in Heaven.

"Yeah, but why are you really here? Why do you believe in this? And who pays for your stay?" she asked.

I stepped forward, feeling the Spirit urging me to share my testimony. "Sister Sandra, this is the Book of Mormon," I said holding it up for her to see. "I have read this book and it changed my life. From its pages, I have come to understand that God not only loves me, but He has a plan for me. This is all possible through Jesus Christ. Once I read this book, I knew I needed to share its teachings with others. Because of that, Elder Pierce and I are paying $400 a month to be here in Singapore. We have sacrificed two years of our lives away from our families, and today we were supposed to meet you."

Sandra took a step back, scratched her arms, and exclaimed, "What am I feeling? Are you wizards or something? Why is my body all tingly?"

I then explained to her that we were not wizards, but that the Holy Spirit carries our "message to the hearts" of those who will listen (*Preach My Gospel*, 3). The Holy Spirit was confirming to her that what I said was true. Sandra was ecstatic. She met with us the following Sunday, came to church, and accepted the invitation to be baptized. She was a "golden" contact.

Sandra promised us she would never miss church. Nevertheless, a few weeks later, her employer made her go to Hong Kong for work (a four-hour flight from Singapore). Being unaware of the situation, no matter how many times we tried to call her, the phone just kept going straight to voicemail. We thought perhaps she had learned something distasteful about the church and we were afraid we would never see or hear from her again.

Sunday came, sacrament meeting began, and Sandra wasn't there. We were distraught. Our first contact with her had been a miracle and we had put so much hope in her. Then, just five minutes into the meeting, we heard the back door open and turned around to see Sandra walking in. *Oh thank goodness,* we thought.

She came and sat by us. "Elders," she said, "I'm so sorry! I saw all your missed calls and texts and couldn't answer because of my employer. But, I promised I would never miss church, so I bought a plane ticket from Hong Kong to Singapore this morning!"

Dakota and I looked at each other in amazement. This lady, not realizing that Hong Kong also had the Church, had literally just bought a plane ticket to attend church. Maybe we were wizards!

We could have easily given up that night in the subway station. With ten minutes of our week left, it would have been easy to throw in the towel and go home. Instead, we sincerely tried to unify ourselves with the Spirit and work hard. It paid off.

Six weeks after meeting Sandra, she was baptized. Today, she remains an active member of the Church in Kharkiv, Ukraine.

Working with the Spirit does include hard work, but "without the Spirit, you will never succeed regardless of your talent and ability" (Ezra Taft Benson, *Preach My Gospel,* 176). Spiritual experiences are what lead to true conversion. No man's persuasion could have convinced Sandra to buy a plane ticket to attend church. Only the Spirit can imprint upon the hearts of those we teach feelings deep enough for any lasting commitment.

Sandra, circled, at her baptism

SOMETIMES WE DON'T KNOW WHY

DAKOTA

Two short stories.

First story. I was biking down the street in the jungle of Kuching, East Malaysia, when I had the strong prompting to stop and talk to a lady unloading a truck along the side of the road. Given my strong spiritual prompting, I anticipated a miracle. I thought for sure God was going to lead me to someone begging to be baptized. To my confusion, this lady was not. She cordially declined the gospel and we went on our way. End of story.

Second story. A man named Keith cleaned the Singapore stake center for twenty years. Missionaries were always doing stuff at the stake center, and so for twenty years missionaries attempted to share the gospel with him in passing. I'm willing to bet that hundreds of missionaries had contacted him. However, he was set in his ways and saw no need for religion in his life.

I was serving in Singapore at the time, when one day, Keith rolled into the Singapore stake center in a wheelchair with only one leg after a recent accident. He rolled right up to me and said, "Elder, I need to be baptized. Please teach me and my wife the gospel."

Two months later, he and his wife were baptized.

Looking back, I feel for the hundreds of missionaries who had unsuccessfully contacted Keith. Perhaps, like me with the lady on the side of the road, they were strongly prompted to share the gospel with him. Perhaps, like me, they had been confused on why they felt prompted to share the gospel with someone who was so uninterested. When we follow the Spirit, sometimes we know why, but sometimes we don't.

The point is to understand that the Holy Ghost is *not* a tool. The Holy Ghost is the boss. Truly, God's ways are higher than our ways (see Isaiah 55:8–9). From our perspective, His higher can look sideways, backward, and upside down, but His perspective is perfect. We are working on ours.

THE HOLY GHOST SAVED MY LIFE

For behold, again I say unto you that if ye will enter in by the way, and receive the Holy Ghost, it will show unto you all things what ye should do. (2 Nephi 32:5)

The Holy Ghost is given unto us. However, it's up to us to let Him into us. If we allow Him into us, He will show us the way, and many times protect us from danger.

MATTHEW

I was serving in west Malaysia in what was considered one of the more "dangerous" cities in the mission—dangerous enough that sisters were currently not allowed to serve there, and the locals sometimes heckled the elders. This was also my first area, so I was new to understanding how the Spirit spoke to me. Oftentimes, I couldn't decide if it was my own thoughts or thoughts from God. (We'll talk more on this later.)

One night, Elder Gunderson and I took the bus to an appointment eight miles away from our apartment. It was late when we finished teaching, and we needed to hurry back for curfew. As we waited at the bus stop, a man approached us and said, "Tiada bus lagi!" ("There are no more buses!")

Discouraged, we began walking home. There was no way we would make it back to our apartment before curfew, but we had no other choice. We had been walking for about fifteen minutes when I looked back and noticed a car slowly driving about 150 feet behind us. "Elder Gunderson," I whispered intensely. "Someone is following us."

"No way," he replied. "They are probably just driving slowly. Let's take a right up here and see what they do."

We took a side road and hoped they would continue on, but our worst fears were confirmed. The car slowly turned right, and now we were in a dimly lit neighborhood.

"Run!" I yelled.

We began sprinting, making our way right, left, straight, and left again to get back to the main road. All of a sudden, I had the impression that we needed to pray and we needed to pray *now*. I grabbed Elder Gunderson and we stood under a streetlamp as I began to pray. "Please Heavenly Father, send us help now. We want to get home safely, and do Thy work!"

As we opened our eyes, a taxi pulled up next to us. The driver rolled down the window and said, "Hey, friend, it's already late. Do you two need a ride back to your house?"

We jumped in the taxi and the suspicious car drove past us. Elder Gunderson and I looked at each other in shock and joy.

President Russell M. Nelson taught, "In coming days, it will not be possible to survive spiritually without the guiding, directing, comforting and constant influence of the Holy Ghost" ("Revelation for the Church, Revelation for Our Lives," *Ensign*, May 2018). In the future, we will all face spiritual, and perhaps even physical, danger. We need to prepare for those situations now by unifying ourselves with the Spirit, because otherwise it might prove too late.

THE ELEVENTH TOE

DAKOTA

Elder Walters and I sat down to teach the less active Gee family for what must've been the fifth time. Not once had they come to church since we taught them. I was beginning to think we were wasting our time.

We began with a prayer, and then I looked down at our lesson plan—the plan of salvation. *Again? I'm pretty sure we taught this to them last time*, I thought. Looking over at Elder Walters, I gave him the go-ahead glance, hoping he could start this lesson. He nodded yes, and I turned to stare out the window as he began . . .

A couple minutes later, I zoned back in. Elder Walters was sitting upright, and I could tell I had missed something important.

". . . and then they just cut off my little brother's toe. Just like that," Elder Walters said.

Confused as to what part of the plan of salvation referred to cutting off toes, I wondered if my companion had gone crazy. Then, out of nowhere, the mom brought their baby daughter out from the bedroom. I was shocked. The mom usually didn't attend our lessons.

"Yeah, actually our baby has an eleventh toe also," the mom said as she slipped off her baby's shoe to show us. "We've been really struggling and praying to know what to do, like whether or not to get it cut off. It's a scary procedure."

My companion and I looked at each other wide-eyed. Then for the next twenty minutes, Elder Walters went into the details of what the procedure was like and the benefits. I just sat there dumbfounded as we taught one of the most powerful plan of salvation lessons I'd ever taught, all focused on my companion's little brother's eleventh toe surgery. I didn't even know eleventh toe surgery was a thing.

As soon as we left their house, I turned to Elder Walters and said, "How'd you know that their baby had the same problem? I don't remember her saying anything about it."

Elder Walters smiled at me. "I didn't know," he said. "It was the weirdest thing, I started talking about the plan of salvation, and then suddenly, I had this feeling that I should talk about my little brother's eleventh toe. So I just went for it, hoping to connect it to the plan of salvation somehow."

"That's insane!" I practically yelled. "We've been together for five months, and you've never said anything to me about your little brother's eleventh toe, and now you bring it up in this random less active member's lesson? What are the chances?"

Elder Walters looked me in the eyes. "Elder Pierce, that wasn't chance. The Holy Ghost doesn't take chances."

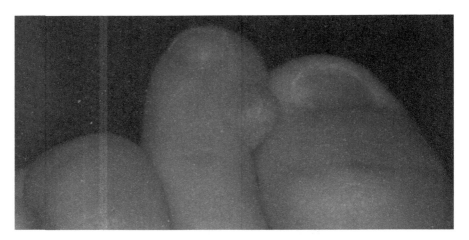

Elder Walters' little brother's eleventh toe

Clearly, Elder Walters had been more in tune with the Spirit that day than I had been. The scriptures promise us that if you "treasure up in your [mind] continually the words of life . . . it shall be given you in the very hour, yea, in the very moment, what ye shall say" (D&C 84:85; D&C 100:6). Treasuring up the words of life does not mean staring out the window during a lesson. It does not mean hanging out with members or rolling out of bed five minutes late and doing your studies in your pajamas.

Treasuring up the words of life means first taking the words of life seriously by recognizing the importance of the gospel and the respect it deserves. For example, "exercise, shower, [eat,] and pray *before* you study" (*Preach My Gospel*, 22; emphasis added). "Study at a desk or table," not lying down or sitting on your bed (*Preach My Gospel*, 22). Have you ever watched President Russell M. Nelson at general conference? Not when he's giving a talk, but when he is sitting on the stand. He sits up straight, on the edge of his chair, and looks out attentively at the audience or the speaker. Have you ever tried that? It's not that easy. President Nelson is doing his best to qualify for the Spirit's guidance by treasuring up the words of life and giving them the respect they deserve.

When God plucks on the strings of our hearts and minds, we must be holding the strings taut. Minimizing the slack in these strings takes consistent daily effort.

Otherwise, we won't feel God's promptings, or perhaps we will attribute them to just another coincidence.

HOW DO I KNOW IF IT'S THE SPIRIT?

Many people wonder how they can know if a thought or feeling is from the Spirit.

DAKOTA

One of the most important things anyone has ever done for me was my youth Sunday School teacher handing me a plain two-dollar composition notebook titled "My Spiritual Journal." Only when I started recording spiritual experiences as a teenager did I begin to recognize the Spirit.

Elder Richard G. Scott taught, "Knowledge carefully recorded is knowledge available in time of need. Spiritually sensitive information should be kept in a sacred place that communicates to the Lord how you treasure it. This practice enhances the likelihood of your receiving further light" ("Acquiring Spiritual Knowledge," *Ensign*, Nov. 1993, 86).

Elder Ronald A. Rasband adds, "We must be confident in our first promptings. Sometimes we rationalize; we wonder if we are feeling a spiritual impression or if it's just our own thoughts. When we begin to second-guess, even third-guess, our feelings—and we all have—we are dismissing the Spirit; we are questioning divine counsel. The prophet Joseph Smith taught if you will listen to the first promptings, you will get it right nine times out of ten" ("Let the Holy Spirit Guide," *Ensign*, May 2017).

As I have read past spiritual experiences and promptings in my spiritual journal, it's easier to recognize God's hand. Nonetheless, don't worry too much about whether it's a spiritual prompting or your own thoughts. According to President Gordon B. Hinckley, the final test is to ask yourself, "Does it persuade one to do good, to rise, to stand tall, to do the right thing, to be kind, to be generous?" (*Teachings of Gordon B. Hinckley*, 260–61). If so, you can push forward, confident that you are following the Spirit.

Throughout the remainder of our book, you will find many stories where we followed the Spirit. Actually, we have entire journals full of spiritual experiences, many of which we haven't and won't share with you. Some are just too personal or sacred, while others would take too long to explain.

Our hope in writing this chapter is not that you will rely solely on our experiences to believe in the Spirit, but that you will begin your own journey to proactively ask for, look for, and recognize the Holy Spirit in your day-to-day life. As you recognize the Spirit in your life, you will begin to naturally share the gospel.

CHALLENGE #4

THROUGHOUT THE COMING WEEK, RECORD IN YOUR SPIRITUAL JOURNAL AT LEAST ONE TIME YOU FELT THE SPIRIT.

HELPFUL SUGGESTIONS

- If you haven't already, buy a small notebook (or start a Google document) and designate it as your spiritual journal (see Nephi and his small vs. large plates in 1 Nephi 9).

- Read *Preach My Gospel,* chapter four, the section titled, "Learn to Recognize the Promptings of the Spirit."

- Read "Receiving, Recognizing, and Responding to the Promptings of the Holy Ghost," Elder David A. Bednar, Ricks College devotional, August 31, 1999. (See www2.byui.edu/Presentations/Transcripts/Devotionals/1999_08_31 _Bednar.htm.)

CHAPTER 5
ATTITUDE IS EVERYTHING

Merriam-Webster.com's definition of attitude:

at·ti·tude—a feeling or emotion toward a fact or [situation]

Matthew and Dakota's definition of attitude:

at·ti·tude—your choice of how you think or feel toward a fact or situation

When it comes down to it, your attitude really is your own choice. You can choose to be happy. You might think your circumstances aren't perfect. You might say, "If only this . . . ," or, "If only that . . . , then I'd be happy." There might be hard things in your life. So go and change them, but don't say you aren't getting what you deserve, because in life, "People do not get what they deserve; life would be hellish if they did . . . God's protection and care come precisely because you do not deserve it and cannot earn it. Grace doesn't come to you because you've performed well on your job or even made great sacrifices as a parent or as a friend. Grace comes to you as part of the gift of being created" (David Brooks, *Road to Character*, 206). And that is why, no matter what, you can choose to be happy.

Regardless of circumstances, there will be hard days—days that you don't want to choose to be happy. Whether they come on your mission or at home, that's normal. That's life. Just knowing Jesus Christ suffered all your "pains and afflictions and temptations" doesn't magically cure all your problems (Alma 7:11). If He did that, then we'd miss the point. He didn't suffer for us so that He could fix our problems for us. He suffered so He could help *us* fix them (see Alma 7:12; "succor," Merriam-Webster.com).

Think of Nephi, when his brothers tied him up in the wilderness (see 1 Nephi 7). Nephi didn't ask God to loosen the bands that held him bound. Rather, he asked God, "Give *me* strength that I may burst these bands" (1 Nephi 7:17; emphasis added). Happiness isn't derived from believing that Christ will change our circumstances but from understanding that He will walk alongside us through every valley of life, succoring us every step of the way (see Alma 7:12).

In other words, we must figuratively "break our own bands" in life instead of waiting for Christ to break them for us. With that in mind, we'd like to suggest a few techniques that might help you choose to be happy every day.

MOTIVATION FOLLOWS ACTION

Have you ever noticed that the first rep at the gym is always the hardest? If you can just get yourself to start, then you tend to finish. If you can just find a way to do ten push-ups or talk to ten people, then doing the next ninety push-ups, or talking to the next ninety people, is relatively easy. Try it. The trick is to choose to fake this positive attitude until you encounter a positive result. After ten push-ups, you will likely feel slightly healthier. After talking to ten strangers about the gospel, you have a better chance of encountering someone who is interested. Then, having seen a positive result, your attitude now not only hinges upon a choice you've made, but it also focuses on your newfound successful experience.

This principle called "motivation follows action" is not restricted to exercising and missionary work. Listed below are some additional examples:

BEFORE YOUR MISSION

- Can't get yourself to read the scriptures? Start by grabbing your scriptures and reading five verses. Chances are, you'll end up reading a chapter.

- Can't get yourself to do your chores? Convince yourself to wash one dish or to pull out the lawnmower. Soon, your chores won't seem so hard.

DURING YOUR MISSION

- Start each day by talking to the first person you see once you're out of the house. You'll probably end up talking to many more.

- Can't get yourself out of bed? Go to the bathroom, get a drink of water, or do a push-up. The bed won't seem as enticing.

Note: We encourage you to try all of these and see what works best for you. You can even create others!

IGNORE THE NEGATIVE AND FOCUS ON THE POSITIVE

We like to refer to this as "Skip (and Flip) Your Negativity."

Let's say you are seeing results that are supporting your positive attitude, but these positive results are more rare than you'd like. For example, instead of finding one person out of ten who is interested in the gospel, you find one for every hundred people. Getting ninety-nine rejections for every one success doesn't sound very fun or effective. So what can you do?

We have two suggestions: First, learn to skip the negativity. Second, flip it into something positive. In other words, ignore the negative and focus on the positive.

Skipping the negativity is a choice you can practice daily, long before you step into the mission field. It's the choice to focus on the positive, no matter how rare it seems to be.

President Gordon B. Hinckley shared a story about reasoning positively:

> Once a man who had been slandered by a newspaper came to [his friend] asking what to do about it. Said [his friend], "Do nothing! Half the people who bought the paper never saw the article, half of those who read it, did not understand it. Half of those who understood it did not believe it. Half of those who believed it are of no account anyway." So many of us make a great fuss of matters of small consequence. We are so easily offended. Happy [and successful] is the [missionary] who can brush aside the offending remarks of another and go on his way. ("Slow to Anger," *Ensign*, Nov. 2007)

Problems arise when we begin to take negative experiences personally. When a rattlesnake bites you, you don't chase after the snake. Instead, you try to get the venom out of your system as fast as possible. If you chase after the snake to get revenge, you will probably die. But if you rush to the hospital and try to get the venom out, you will probably live. The same occurs in our daily interactions with people. Most likely the snake that bit you, the companion or friend who gossiped behind your back, or the stranger who rejected your offer of the Book of Mormon, was not intentionally trying to hurt you. Rather, they were just doing what they thought was in their own best interest. It's your choice to let it affect your attitude.

Another less obvious (but just as demeaning) way of taking negative experiences personally is to compare yourself to others. Think back to when Jesus Christ and the two thieves were crucified. Many people found joy in following the triple execution, because by witnessing their fellows suffer, they felt better about themselves (see Talmage, *Jesus The Christ*, 652). We may be more like these witnesses than we care to admit. This type of comparison provides only temporary contentment and does not help us develop the pure love of Christ. Practice finding happiness in others' successes and sadness in their sufferings (see Mosiah 18:9).

Even in basketball, where the goal is to be better than the other team, the famous basketball coach John Wooden taught what he learned from his father: "Don't worry much about trying to be better than someone else. Learn from others, yes. But don't just try to be better than they are. You have no control over that. Instead try, and try very hard, to be the best that you can be. That, you have control over" (as quoted by Joseph B. Wirthlin in "One Step after Another," *Ensign*, Nov. 2001; see also John Wooden, *A Lifetime of Observations and Reflections On and Off the Court*).

While choosing to skip our negative experiences is good, we should also be choosing to flip our negative experiences by learning from them. For example, if you talk to a hundred people on the street, and ninety-nine reject you, is it enough to just admit that the ninety-nine are doomed for hell and there is nothing you can do about it? No! Instead, learn something from them. Think about your approach for introducing the gospel to these ninety-nine people and how and why they might have rejected you. Then, alter or restructure your approach to see if your outcome can be improved. Most important, pray to your Father in Heaven and ask for strength in overcoming discouragement. Ask Him what approach He would have you take. It's His work, after all. He will know how you can have the greatest success in whatever you do. After you pray, listen and follow the promptings you receive. If you don't flip your negative experiences into constructive improvements through critical thinking and talking with the Lord, your rate of success will rarely change.

DAKOTA

When I first began my mission, I tried to teach the whole first lesson (covering the restoration) in my first meeting with new people. While this yielded some success, it also resulted in many people canceling their future appointments. At first I decided to only skip these negative experiences and not take the time to understand why so many people opted to stop meeting with us. Then, I decided to flip these negative experiences into a constructive improvement. After some thought and prayer, I realized that many of the people we taught had limited, if any, Christian background. With this in mind, I began to teach the plan of salvation in the first lesson, or even just who God is and how to communicate with Him. It quickly became clear that this tailored approach was much more effective in connecting with and retaining the people we taught. (See "Fundamentals from *Preach My Gospel*: Teach People Not Lessons," missionary.org.)

CHANGE YOUR EXPECTATIONS, CHANGE YOUR REALITY

Any attitude contains some level of expectations. Whether it be a job interview, a missionary discussion, or a dinner table chat with your family, the type of expectations that you believe are reasonable usually are. This is because what you expect to happen usually ends up happening. Healthy expectations, however, are not usually found within the bounds of our comfort zones.

MATTHEW

I had just been transferred from Malaysia to Singapore, and Elder Fair and I would be companions for the day. According to the mission president, he had been struggling to find new people to teach, and his attitude wasn't the best. When I arrived at his apartment, we started planning for the day. I could tell he was struggling, because mid-planning he exclaimed, "Elder Spurrier, Singapore is just not like Malaysia. We don't find people here!"

"Elder Fair," I responded, "how many people interested in the gospel do you believe God can help us find tomorrow?"

"Five people would be a stretch," he said.

"How about fifty?" I asked. I'm pretty sure his jaw hit the floor in shock, but I was serious.

"Fifty?" he said. "No way. Impossible."

Two minutes later, we had compromised on a goal of finding twenty-five people interested in the gospel who were willing to give us their address or phone number for future appointments. Nevertheless, I could tell he didn't actually believe we would reach our goal.

That day was full of miracles, but one contact stood out among the rest. As we were riding on the train, we began talking with a woman and explaining why we were in Singapore.

"Sister!" I said, grinning. "We are here to share a message of joy—that Christ died for us, and His gospel can bring us more happiness and peace than anything else in this world!"

Elder Fair stood there expecting another rejection, a blank look on his face. She listened to what we had to say, but as the train stopped, she pointed at me and said, "Well, you seem to believe this message can bring you joy, but—" she turned and pointed at Elder Fair "—your friend here doesn't. I'll have to pass."

Elder Fair was shocked. He turned to me and asked, "Is my attitude affecting the work that much?"

Matthew happily sharing the gospel on the train

By the end of the day, we had found exactly twenty-five interested people. We had lots of laughs, and Elder Fair had made plans to change his expectations and attitude toward the Lord's work no matter where he served.

Many of you will be called to missions in South America or Africa where the attitude and expectation is to teach lots of lessons and baptize loads of people. Some of you will be called to Europe, Asia, or other places, and as you arrive, you will hear, "This isn't South America or Africa. We don't baptize as much." The secret is you can have success (whether it's baptisms, reactivating less active members, or serving others) no matter where you go, in every area you serve. We have noticed that missionaries who hold this perspective have more success than those who don't. There is no such thing as a "bad area." There might be "harder areas," but there are no "bad areas." Besides, wouldn't you rather be known as the missionary who changed a "hard area" rather than another lucky missionary who got an "easy area?" (See *Preach My Gospel*, "Developing the Faith to Find," 155; *A Successful Missionary*, 10).

Someone in a press conference once asked President Spencer W. Kimball what he did when he was in a boring sacrament meeting. He replied, "I don't know. I've never been in one" (Ted Barnes, "How to Never Have a Boring Church Class Ever Again," *New Era*, Jan. 2013). President Kimball was an expert at taking advantage of the situations he found himself in. He found reasons to be there by having positive expectations. So, if you think you have a "hard area" or your mission is "boring," think again.

When developing your expectations, start by praying and asking the Lord what His expectations are for you (at any given point in time). Tell Him your goals and ask Him what He would have you do. Listen to the Spirit and follow the promptings you receive. Questions to evaluate your expectations include, "What are the Lord's expectations for you?" "How can you align your will with God's will?" "How have you seen the Lord's hand in your work so far?"

Listed below are some examples to help you practice setting your expectations:

- Mentally picture the people you meet and teach dressed in white, in the baptismal font, or in the temple (even the people you meet on the street).

- When impressed, invite those you are teaching to read more than what is assigned and see if they can take that challenge. (For example, ask people to read the entire book of 3 Nephi instead of just 3 Nephi 11.)

Note: We acknowledge that smaller, more manageable expectations can also be effective; however, these smaller expectations often lead to complacency.

YOU GET WHAT YOU REALLY WANT

Elder Christofferson once came to our mission and told us flatly, "You get what you really want." He then paused and repeated, "You get what you really want." Truly, our inner desires have a huge impact on who we become and what we accomplish.

Jesus taught,

If a son shall ask bread of any of you that is a father, will he give him a stone? or if he ask a fish, will he for a fish give him a serpent?

Or if he shall ask an egg, will he offer him a scorpion?

If ye then, being evil, know how to give good gifts unto your children: how much more shall your heavenly Father give...to them that ask him? (Luke 11:11–13)

DAKOTA

Before I submitted my mission papers, I remember thinking and praying, "Heavenly Father, I'm willing to serve anywhere, so no matter where I am sent, I will be ready!" And I felt good about that. I was willing to serve anywhere, and I was excited to see where God needed me.

Soon after I offered this prayer, I realized that my dad was not on the same page. As I mentioned earlier, he was a convert and hadn't served a mission. One day as we were talking on the phone, he told me, "If you get called to an English-speaking mission, I will personally call the prophet and get it changed. You need to learn Chinese."

Although I wasn't sure if he was serious, he sounded serious at the time, and my dad isn't someone who messes around with stuff like that. I remember talking with my bishop about it and struggling to balance honoring my parents and honoring God. It wasn't as simple as just pleasing or displeasing either of them. I also had three younger siblings, and I knew that if my mission failed in any way, the chances of my dad supporting them to serve would drop catastrophically. However, a successful mission from my dad's point of view would probably guarantee his support of my siblings serving as well. With the help of my bishop, my dad and I decided to write a little note on my application saying, "I would welcome the opportunity to serve in a Chinese-speaking mission if there are any available."

Even after studying Spanish for three years in high school, to my surprise, two months later, I was called to the Mandarin Chinese-speaking Singapore Mission. Yes, my dad was ecstatic. My mission was a success, and my younger brother successfully served his mission in Taiwan, which is also a Chinese-speaking mission.

Dakota's family reunited after both he and his little brother had returned from their Mandarin Chinese-speaking missions

We've heard other similar stories as well. Gordon B. Hinckley, who was an Apostle at the time, interviewed a Malaysian member's father for his mission. (Prospective missionaries used to be interviewed by Apostles.) During the interview, Elder Hinckley asked him, "Where would you like to serve?"

He responded, "Well, not in North or South America, but somewhere in between."

Elder Hinckley looked at him and chuckled. "That sounds like Central America?"

The member's father nodded. "Yes."

A few weeks later, he received his mission call to what was, at the time, called the Central America Mission.

God doesn't always call us to serve in places for specific reasons other than the fact that He wants to see what we will make happen with the opportunity we are given, and He wants to honor our desires. So take whatever calling, area assignment, job, class, or anything else you are given and make it great (see Matthew 25:21).

DAKOTA

People often ask me, "How'd you get accepted into MIT? You must be a genius!" Or, "How'd you get an internship at NASA and Apple? How did they find you?" The truth is, they never found me. I found them. In fact, I'm not a genius. I just understood what I wanted and then asked for it! I was the one who emailed the head basketball coach at MIT asking to be recruited, and I was the one who emailed NASA and Apple employees asking for an internship. No one ever came looking for me. When desire and hard work align, asking makes all the difference. Unless you ask, the answer is always no!

JUST ASK? THAT'S IT?

When Elder Christofferson said, "You get what you want," he didn't mean just ask for it. Asking is generally the last step. If you genuinely want something, you will work for it. Otherwise, you don't really want it.

When Joseph Smith successfully tested James's promise, "If any of you lack wisdom, let him ask of God," nothing was easy (James 1:5). Joseph pondered and read his scriptures consistently. He struggled with deciding on a church to attend. He did his background research. Then, he chose a day, time, and place to pray. When he prayed, the adversary bombarded him. He prayed vocally but felt the devil bind his tongue and spread darkness over him. Only when Joseph felt "ready to sink into despair and abandon [himself] to destruction" did God finally give "liberally, and upbraideth not" (Joseph Smith—History 1:16; James 1:5). Had Joseph given up on James's promise at any point in this process, where would we be today?

Like Joseph, if what you want is something that you've never had, there is a good chance you'll have to do what you've never done.

WHAT IF YOU ASK AND DON'T RECEIVE?

Christ asks, "If a son shall ask bread of any of you that is a father, will he give him a stone?" (Luke 11:11). This infers that your Father in Heaven knows how to give the best gifts. Sometimes we ask for bread, and God gives us a banana. And sometimes in the moment, that banana can seem like a stone, because maybe we hate bananas. But God knows that what we really need is vitamin B, and we just don't realize it. We must learn to trust Him, and we must learn to be better askers.

MATTHEW

Although Dakota asked to serve a Chinese-speaking mission and was blessed to receive that call, I was not.

I had taken two years of Chinese in high school. I wanted to serve internationally, and I explicitly wrote on my mission application that I would love to serve in a Chinese-speaking mission. When I opened my call and saw "Singapore Mission, Malay-speaking," I was grateful that God had answered part of my prayer, but confused why he hadn't answered the rest.

In the moment, it was hard to swallow that banana. I really wanted bread. You could say it felt that I had received a stone. However, looking back, it's easy to see why God wanted me to speak Malay. I could write an entire book on why, but, suffice it to say, the people I met and relationships I developed led to more miracles than I thought possible. Then, after returning home, I was blessed to support Malay translation and interpretation for the Church since Malay is still a relatively primitive language in the Church.

Sometimes God will answer your prayers exactly the way you ask. Sometimes He will give you the bread you ask for. At times, He has done so for me. Other times, He has given me something unexpected. Nonetheless, you can trust that He always has the bigger picture in mind. (See "The Will of God," ChurchofJesusChrist.org; "God is the Gardener," Hugh B. Brown, BYU Speeches.) The truth is, you get what you really want, but not always in the way you want it. For me, I realized that what I really wanted was to impact the most people that I could, in the deepest way I could, through the gospel. I got that 100 percent.

WHAT IF NOTHING WORKS? WHAT THEN?

What if nothing works? What happens if you are choosing the greatest attitude combined with the most faith-filled actions, and yet no tangible success or green lights seem to appear? What happens if this becomes a pattern and, like Job and Joseph Smith, you feel all hell descending upon you and the powers of the devil working against you in full force? (See Joseph Smith—History 1; Job 10.) What then?

In these moments, it's healthy to question who or what your faith is really in. Is it in success and green lights? Is it in baptizing and numerical success? Is it in physical milestones? Or is it in the Savior and His plan? Miracles follow true disciples of Jesus Christ, but that doesn't mean we will win every battle. God's plan for us has a happy-ever-after ending, but that doesn't mean it won't be full of mountains and valleys. Your story will likely end with eternal life, but that doesn't mean it will be all green lights to the finish line. Likely, you'll encounter more red lights than green. Your job is to focus on the green.

When we arrive at the judgment bar, many people may want to throw their spiritual résumés at Christ's feet. They might want to claim how many baptisms they had, how many goals they hit, or how much service they provided. In these instances, Christ may very well respond, "I never knew you: depart from me, ye that work iniquity" (Matthew 7:23). "Ultimately, no one will be able to compile a résumé that is able to please God and provide confidence. Instead, our only hope is that Jesus has promised salvation to anyone who repents of sin and trusts in Him" (Michael Mckinley, *Am I Really Christian?*).

This realization shouldn't stop us from "baptiz[ing] nations," helping members, providing service, or working toward goals, but rather help us recognize our dependence upon Christ (Matthew 18:19). Without Him, there is no reason to write any résumé. "Choose faith in [Christ], not results" (Mary Stallings, Instagram, @comefollowme-daily, 2019).

A good attitude is not just something you can work on behaviorally. Behavioral training can help, but only a hope in Christ can fully change the attitude of our natures. When we focus on the doctrine of Christ, we can become hopeful in Him. "The unfailing source of hope is that we are sons and daughters of God and that His Son, the Lord Jesus Christ, saved us from death" (*Preach My Gospel*, 117). "The attitude you have toward your mission experience is a reflection of your love toward your Heavenly Father and His Son" (*Preach My Gospel*, 151).

STAYING MENTALLY SANE

After talking to you for an entire chapter about having a positive attitude, we also want you to understand that missions can be stressful and hard. Missionary work can exhaust you, drain you emotionally and spiritually, provoke self-doubt, and sometimes just cause our brains to feel out of whack. Why is this?

The Cleveland Clinic states that "stress is a normal reaction the body has when changes occur. It can respond to these changes physically, mentally, or emotionally" (Cleveland Clinic, "Stress"). Feeling stressed is normal, especially because on a mission your environment, companion, language needs, and area are often changing all the time. As soon as you start feeling comfortable in a routine, companionship, or area, things change, and you might have to start all over. In some ways, your mission is eighteen to twenty-four months of constant change. No wonder it's easy to become stressed and anxious. "Sometimes a mission feels like a wonderful spiritual adventure—or at least a challenge you can handle . . . At other times, however, you may face unexpected problems or experiences that are more difficult or unpleasant than you anticipated" (*Adjusting to Missionary Life*, "Understanding Stress," 5).

When Christ prepared to leave the Apostles, you can imagine that they were probably pretty stressed. The Savior and Master Teacher was leaving, and it was their turn to run the Church, teach the masses, and correct false doctrine. In response to their nerves, the Savior said, "And I will pray the Father, and he shall give you another Comforter, that he may abide with you forever; . . . I will not leave you comfortless: I will come to you" (John 14:16, 18). The Holy Ghost will strengthen your resolve and aid you during stressful times. For more spiritual, physical, social, and emotional stress-relieving techniques, please read *Adjusting to Missionary Life* on ChurchofJesusChrist.org.

Missions are very difficult at times. You may find yourself more stressed than you have ever been before. Along with diligent prayer, the *Adjusting to Missionary Life* book released by the Church can help you stay on your mission and stay mentally sane, like it did for us. Next to *Preach My Gospel* and the scriptures, we vouch for that book being the most instructive and useful book for missionaries. Use the suggestions it provides. They really do help.

CHALLENGE #5

DEVELOP A HEALTHY MENTAL ATTITUDE

PLEASE CHOOSE AND COMMIT TO ONE OF THE FOLLOWING ACTIVITIES

HELPFUL SUGGESTIONS

- Pray daily for the gift of a positive attitude.
- Begin a gratitude journal.
- Take the self-assessment record on page 12 of *Adjusting to Missionary Life*, ChurchofJesusChrist.org.
- Talk to God about the worst part of your day. Find His hand in it.
- Begin a weekly journal.
- Repeat out loud a daily positive affirmation, such as "I will have a positive attitude today!"
- Say a daily prayer where you only tell God things you are grateful for.

CHAPTER 6
TALKING TO STRANGERS

rowing up, your mom probably told you, "Never talk to strangers!" And right-fully so: her job is to keep you safe. However, this is the opposite of good mission preparation, because on a mission, your job is to talk with strangers all day long. *Preach My Gospel*, chapter nine, has a section titled "Talking With Everyone." "Everyone" predominantly includes strangers.

WHAT IF I'M NOT GOOD AT TALKING OR DON'T LIKE IT?

DAKOTA

Before my mission, public speaking was not my thing. I cringed anytime I had to give a sacrament meeting talk and usually read directly from a script. Making eye contact with an audience felt unbearable. I enjoyed spending time by myself in my own room. I was scared to even say "hi" to my neighbors. You might feel the same. Like I did, you might find yourself thinking, "How in the world am I supposed to follow *Preach My Gospel* and talk with everyone?" (see *Preach My Gospel*, 156). Nevertheless, despite my doubts, I became an extrovert on my mission. It was a slow process, and I'd be lying if I said it was easy. I really struggled at first. I soon learned that like the prophets Moses and Enoch, you don't have to be good at speaking to carry forth God's work (see Moses 6:31; Exodus 4:10–12). You just have to be willing to try. You'll probably mess up many times, and that's okay. I did! That's how we learn.

On my very first day in the mission field, I was excited to share the gospel but was not talented or skilled at doing so. We had one lesson planned for that afternoon. I had learned about the sticks of Joseph and Judah during personal study that morning and wanted to share it for our lesson (Ezekiel 37:16–20). I still don't understand why I thought it was a good idea to focus on such a complicated analogy in a first lesson with someone we had never met, but I did. Whatever my reasoning was, my trainer told me that he would let me take the lead for our first lesson, and I was ecstatic.

However, when I began the lesson, I realized what a high level of Bible background knowledge was necessary to actually relate with the analogy of the sticks of Joseph and Judah. On top of that, with my minimal Chinese, it took me five minutes to read Ezekiel 37:16–20 out loud to her, without even beginning to explain it. During my language study that morning, I had learned how to say "stick" in Chinese to prepare to teach this lesson. During my attempted explanation of the scripture, I probably repeated the word "stick" twenty-five times. Each time I said the word "stick" the expression on her face told me she understood less.

Here I was, in the middle of the jungle in East Malaysia, teaching a lady who I wasn't sure could even read or write about the sticks of Judah and Joseph, all in a language I could hardly speak and surely couldn't understand.

After ten minutes of struggling, my trainer jumped in to save the day. Even with my trainer salvaging what he could from the lesson, I remember returning to our apartment that night distraught, wondering if I would ever be good at sharing what I believed. However, I refused to let that experience deter me.

I prayed for strength, and just like God did for Moses and Enoch, He molded me. Over the next six months, I learned how to hold good conversations and have effective lessons. Soon, we had five baptisms. The branch hadn't had a baptism for two years, but now it was burning with missionary fire.

Brigham Young once said, "If all the talent, tact, wisdom, and refinement of the world had been sent to me with the Book of Mormon, and had declared, in the most exalted of earthly eloquence, the truth of it, undertaking to prove it by learning and worldly wisdom, they would have been to me like smoke which arises only to vanish away. But when I saw a man without eloquence or talents for public speaking, who could only say, 'I know by the power of the Holy Ghost that the Book of Mormon is true, that Joseph Smith is a Prophet of the Lord,' the Holy Ghost proceeding from that individual illuminated my understanding . . . and I knew for myself that the testimony of the man was true" (*Journal of Discourses*, 1:90).

Although I learned how to hold good conversations and effective lessons, our success certainly had nothing to do with our companionship's talent in speaking the language, or in sharing the gospel. As much as I wanted to be the wise teacher with eloquent words, examples and lessons, I'll be the first to admit that our companionship's "speech and . . . preaching was not with enticing words of man's wisdom, but in demonstration of the Spirit" (1 Corinthians 2:4).

Don't worry about being talented at speaking or if talking to strangers doesn't come naturally. God knows you, and He will mold you if you turn to Him and don't give up. Failure is just a stepping-stone to success.

If anyone needed to understand these principles, it was President Thomas S. Monson. After being called to be an Apostle at age thirty-six, there is no doubt that he felt overwhelmed and underqualified. During his time as president, he often taught two principles in the temple to the Apostles and other General Authorities. First, God qualifies those whom he calls. Second, when you are on the Lord's errand, you are entitled to the Lord's help (Elder Brent H. Nielson, fireside, 2015).

God will bless you. You will get plenty of practice speaking. As crazy as it sounds, talking to strangers will become normal. We got to the point where it felt awkward for us not to stop and talk to strangers. Even today, as returned missionaries, we still feel awkward if we don't greet people in elevators or strike up conversations with our Uber drivers. Eventually, you won't want a single person to walk by without stopping and talking to them. Each person is a child of God, with the potential to be a future god or goddess who can create worlds. Given this, how can you not stop that stranger on the street?

HOW DO I START A CONVERSATION?

Practice making eye contact with people anytime you're walking down the street, down the aisle in a grocery store, or anywhere else in public. Think about how you could start a conversation. What could you say to them?

Unless you are a natural social butterfly, this will feel awkward and outside your comfort zone. Starting a conversation, especially with a stranger, can be intimidating. What do you say to start? Then, how do you keep the conversation going if you don't know what to say next? And, most important, how do you find out about a complete stranger's life challenges without sounding like a creep?

Every missionary struggles with these valid questions. You will develop your own unique style based on personal preference and cultural background, but regardless of your mojo (or lack thereof), the key is to keep trying new techniques until you find something you consider natural and effective.

Below are some techniques that we have found effective for (1) starting a conversation, (2) keeping the conversation going when you don't know what to say next, and (3) transitioning to a discussion of someone's personal struggles and how the gospel fits in.

STARTING A CONVERSATION

- Smile and make eye contact with people (remember, happiness is attractive).
- Compliment people. (You can start simple, such as, "I like your shoes. Do you mind if I ask where you bought them?")
- Ask for directions—it's okay to ask questions you already know the answer to. God does (see Genesis 3:9).
- Offer small acts of service—carry someone's groceries, help someone with yard work, and so on. (See "Go About Doing Good," *Preach My Gospel*, 168.)
- Ask them to take a survey—design a questionnaire that leads into the gospel and ask people if they have a couple minutes to take your small survey.

KEEPING A CONVERSATION GOING

- Begin sharing your own story—people are generally interested in what you are doing and why you decided to come to their area. This should be more personal and natural than "We are missionaries for The Church of . . ," but more along the lines of your story, such as, "I just graduated from high school in Idaho and now I am here in Florida giving up the prime years of my life, all because I felt God talk to me through the Book of Mormon, and I want to share that with you."
- Ask a question—it sounds simple, but people love to talk about themselves, so asking almost any question usually works. (You can also commit to memory several simple go-to questions that you can ask when you don't know what to say next, such as "Where are you from?")
- Ask follow-up questions—a conversation feels less like an interview and more natural when you ask follow-up questions. (An example would be that after you ask, "Where are you from?" don't change the subject, but instead, say, "Nice! Did you enjoy growing up there?")

TRANSITIONING TO A DISCUSSION OF SOMEONE'S PERSONAL STRUGGLES AND HOW THE GOSPEL FITS IN

- Talk with people about their families—this can lead to more personal topics and even family history opportunities (see *Preach My Gospel*, 157).
- Be vulnerable and share some of your own personal struggles—this will encourage strangers to share theirs as well. (It might be hard to think about them in the moment, so consider making a list of several you can share.)

- Offer to say a prayer for them—before you offer the prayer, ask what you can pray for in their life. (This can appropriately take place in most public places, like in the street, in someone's front yard, or at the store.)

We have found these few techniques to be effective. You can try them, but feel free to use new ideas.

The only thing we ask you *not* to do is to develop the habit of walking up to people and asking, "Do you have a few minutes that we could teach you a message about . . . ?" (see *Preach My Gospel*, 159). That's like asking for a down payment on a house without letting the buyer take a tour first. No one wants to do that. Instead, just strike up a conversation and begin sharing gospel truths in natural ways.

Finally, when you talk with people, don't just talk about how the sky is blue and isn't that cool (unless the Spirit prompts you to). Invite them to come unto Christ, find out how the gospel could benefit their individual lives, and give them a specific commitment. *Preach My Gospel* teaches that "rarely, if ever, should you talk to people . . . without extending an invitation to do something that will strengthen their faith in Christ" (196). Don't just shoot the breeze with people. You are a missionary with Jesus Christ's name on your chest. People expect you to talk with them about Jesus.

Remember, people are amazing, and we are all one big happy family. It should be more awkward to *not* talk to your fellow brothers and sisters on the street, not the other way around. C. S. Lewis said, "You have never [met] a mere mortal . . . it is immortals [our spiritual brothers and sisters] whom we joke with, work with, marry, snub and exploit" (*The Weight of Glory*, 45–46). Every person you meet is interesting. If you don't think so, you just don't know them well enough, which is your problem, not theirs.

Getting to know people is fun, because everyone has unique backgrounds, needs, and yearnings. As you become fascinated by each person's journey to know Christ, missionary work becomes enjoyable. People may be shocked by your genuine fascination and excitement over their lives, but they will love it.

TALKING IS BEST INITIATED THROUGH GIVING

Talking to strangers about the gospel can be scary, but it doesn't always have to be initiated through an abrupt street conversation. In fact, it doesn't have to start with talking at all. Giving is a great conversation starter.

Service helps soften the hearts of those around us to hear the gospel. So how do you serve strangers? It can help to think about what you like to do. Do you play sports? Do you cook? Do you ride a unicycle? Play an instrument? Often, these hobbies and talents are overlooked on missions, even though they could be some of our greatest tools to engage people's interest in the gospel.

MATTHEW

Various times throughout my mission, I was able to play the guitar for others, sometimes even large groups of people. It was fun using a talent from home to get people's attention, and then afterward be able to exclaim, "We are missionaries from Christ's restored Church, here to share a message of peace, love, and joy!"

Matthew playing guitar for a group of Malaysian teenagers on preparation day

DAKOTA

With the permission of my mission president, I started a basketball class. It was a huge success, and we even gave everyone jerseys. One of my students was eventually baptized!

Dakota's basketball class in Malaysia

Even if it isn't playing the guitar or teaching basketball, God has given each of us unique talents. Be creative and utilize your gifts to embrace the awkwardness of opening your mouth to share the gospel. With the permission of your mission president, think outside the box to make talking to strangers fun! Some other examples include,

- Start an English class
- Begin a food drive
- Hold a cooking class
- Promote a service project
- Draw the plan of salvation on the ground in chalk in a busy public place
- Set up a stand about the Church (You can offer free listening, consulting, or life coaching.)

AWKWARDNESS IS AWESOME

Some awkwardness is unavoidable. Once you learn to expect some amount of awkwardness when talking to strangers, you'll slowly internalize that awkwardness is a fundamental part of missionary life, and it's *awesome*. In addition, God commands us to "open our mouths" and "fear not" (D&C 33:10; 6:36). To lose your fear, all you need to do is learn how to embrace and expect awkwardness.

Maybe you're thinking that there's no way to make the awkwardness fun. We thought that at first too, but, believe it or not, there are ways to do this. We'd like to share two. First, ask to sit down and eat meals with strangers in public. Second, pray with people you meet in the street or on their doorstep—or anywhere else for that matter.

ARE MEALS BREAK TIME?

Many missionaries consider meals a break time. If you need a break, then certainly take one, but don't let complacency or awkwardness become your excuse.

DAKOTA

One day, we didn't have any specific plans for lunch, so we decided to go to the local food court. Once we had gotten our food, I turned to my companion, Elder Clarke, and said, "Let's sit with that woman for lunch," and I urged him toward a lady sitting in the back corner.

He gave me a ghost face like I was crazy and said, "No, let's not bother her."

I persisted, and we walked over.

"Hi, can we eat with you?" I asked.

Looking up at us, she responded, "Of course! I've been looking for church people like you!"

To our amazement, she then explained that she had been praying for missionaries to come and explain to her the difference between all the churches. Elder Clarke was dumbfounded. Knowing we had exactly the answers to her questions, we went right ahead and shared Joseph Smith's First Vision over hamburgers. I couldn't help but laugh inside as I watched Elder Clarke's jaw drop further and further throughout our "lunch lesson."

We could have kept to ourselves and ate a peaceful, quiet lunch alone, but because we were diligent, we found a miracle. Treat each minute of the day as a golden opportunity to represent your Savior, even during meal times. Matthew and I even had one day where the strangers we sat down to eat with paid for our lunches, three times in a row! I'm pretty sure we tried everything on the menu that day. Sometimes, boldness pays off in ways you wouldn't expect.

PRAYING WITH STRANGERS

Hearing someone pray and talk to God for the first time is an unbelievable experience and never gets old. To help you understand how to effectively encourage someone to pray for the first time after just meeting them on the street or at their doorstep, we've outlined a few critical steps below.

First, ask if they are Christian.

If they are not Christian, then just explain who you are as missionaries and ask if you can say a quick prayer for them. Most people won't turn down the opportunity to have a prayer offered in their behalf. Then, before you offer the prayer, ask if there is anything you can specifically pray for in their or their family member's lives.

Next, offer a heartfelt prayer in their behalf.

After you pray, ask them if they would be willing to pray for you, their kids, or anything else they feel they need. Most people will be hesitant because it's their first time praying, but be persistent and say, "Don't worry. It's easy. Let me teach you!" Then teach them the simple steps of prayer and ask, "Okay! Will you give it a try? Don't worry, there is no right or wrong prayer!" With this type of encouragement and simplicity, we found that a surprisingly large number of people will usually be willing.

On the other hand, if they are Christian, we've found a slightly different approach works better.

After finding out that they are Christian, first ask, "Have you already prayed today?" Most of the time they will not have, and then you can say, "Well, now is a great time! Would you say a prayer with us? Would you mind offering it?"

MATTHEW

I remember being companions with Elder Jackson, an energetic new missionary. He wanted to learn how to better talk to strangers, and I promised him I would do my best to push him out of his comfort zone and teach him some new ways to bring the Spirit into his conversations.

As the day went on, we had our fair share of stopping mopeds to share the gospel with their drivers, sitting with strangers at lunch, and asking every single person we talked with if they had any friends who would like to learn more about Jesus Christ. Later, we felt prompted to go knock on a few doors in a specific apartment complex, but no one seemed to be home. Finally, after knocking a few doors, an Indian woman answered. She told us she was somewhat Christian, so I urged Elder Jackson to ask, "Well, have you prayed today, ma'am?"

"No, not yet," she replied.

Even though I knew it would be uncomfortable for Elder Jackson, I felt prompted, so I locked eyes with the woman and asked, "Would you step outside and pray with us?"

Elder Jackson looked at me in shock. I just grinned at him, trusting the Spirit. The woman paused and then said, "Why not?"

She stepped outside her door, and there, in the middle of the walkway, she said a heartfelt prayer to her Father in Heaven. The Spirit was strong, and we were able to get her phone number after the prayer so we could return and teach her a lesson. As we walked away, Elder Jackson turned, looked at me, and said, "That was crazy, Elder."

It was crazy, but it worked. She had felt the Spirit, and that was all that mattered.

During our missions, using these exact same tactics, we helped hundreds of people pray for the first time on the streets of Malaysia and Singapore.

Even after our missions, we have helped other people pray in places such as Temple Square. We taught these principles to Dakota's younger brother and helped him (who didn't speak Chinese at the time) encourage Chinese tourists at Temple Square to pray for the first time. (See the following photo.)

Dakota, left, Matthew, right, and Dakota's brother, center, teach Chinese tourists how to pray at Temple Square

The secret of talking to strangers is to just push yourself outside your comfort zone. The point is not to force someone to pray, or to sit through an awkward lunch with a stranger. The point is to encourage a spiritual experience. The reason we focus on awkwardness being awesome is that we have come to learn that there is no growth in the comfort zone, and no comfort in the growth zone. When you (or the strangers you talk to) are in the comfort zone, you rely on yourself. However, when you (or the strangers you talk to) get out of the comfort zone, you learn to rely on the Lord.

Your goal should always be to have spiritual experiences with people, not to get their phone number or check the baptismal box. Real fun and success lies in spiritual experiences. These experiences tend to occur more commonly outside of the comfort zone.

ASK FOR REFERRALS FROM *EVERYONE*

Whether people are interested in the gospel or not, we should ask for referrals from everyone (see *Preach My Gospel*, inside back cover). Once that is solidified in your head, the next logical thought is how to ask. You can just plainly ask people if they have friends interested in your message, but it can be helpful to be more specific. You can try asking, "Do you know of anyone who has recently had a baby? Or moved into the area? Or experienced a death in their family?" (See *Preach My Gospel*, 167.) People experiencing these life-changing events are often the most approachable and open to the Spirit and your message.

Furthermore, don't fall into the trap of thinking that asking people for referrals drives the Spirit away. Whether people are interested in your message or not, we promise that politely asking for referrals will never drive the Spirit away.

For people who decline your invitation to learn the gospel, it's easy to believe that they won't want to share your message, but it could be that these same uninterested people have a grandma or son going through a hard time and are begging for meaning to their life. You just don't know, so ask.

For people who do accept your message, it's just as important to ask. People like to share what they think is cool. As missionaries, however, sometimes we think like this: "Oh, 'so-and-so' is so interested. Let's not mess it up by asking them for their friends. They might get offended, and we don't want to drive away the Spirit."

DAKOTA

I once prayed with a lady on the sidewalk and then proceeded to help her pray for the first time in her life. It was an amazing experience, and she was what we call a "golden contact." So golden, in fact, that we almost asked her to be baptized right then and there, but decided to hold back until we met again later that week. As we were walking away, I stopped, remembering that we hadn't asked her to refer any of her friends. I then asked myself, "Do I really want to ruin this amazing experience by asking her for her friends?" Thankfully, I immediately realized I was falling into the natural man's thought process.

I walked back to the side of the road where she was sitting and asked, "Hey! Do you have any friends that you think would also be interested in this message?"

She looked up at me and smiled. "Well," she said, "I think everyone should hear this message." She took out her phone and shared with us the phone numbers of her entire contact list. We were flabbergasted. Forty-three names and phone numbers later, we had to stop her because we realized this wasn't much better than using a phone book with anyone and everyone's phone number in it. She then narrowed the list down to a few people she thought would be seriously interested, and we took down those names and numbers.

Asking this lady to refer her friends not only didn't ruin the spiritual experience we had praying together, it also deepened it. Just as you will come closer to Christ by sharing the gospel, others will as well.

We know that when people are touched by your message and feel the Spirit, they are all the more likely to share it. The idea that asking people to refer their friends drives the Spirit away is just not true.

GOD'S FRIENDS

In our experience, people don't refer the best people. God refers the best people. Unlike us, God is friends with everyone, whether they like it or not. Plus, He knows where everyone is at every moment. You could say that He has the ultimate GPS tracker.

For example, a guy offered us a ride home when he saw us stranded in the rain. He was baptized six weeks later.

Once, a Korean girl ran up to us in a mall and asked, "What church do you go to? Can I come?" She was baptized three months later.

Another time, we had an inactive member randomly bring a friend to church. Even though we never saw the inactive member again, the friend was baptized.

Some of the most receptive people we taught on our missions (baptized or not) were referred from God. There is no other explanation. Having faith in God and Jesus Christ—knowing that they can "refer" people to you who are prepared to learn the gospel—can keep you going through your hardest days and weeks.

DAKOTA

Elder Free and I had set a goal to get fifty phone numbers in a week from people who were interested in the gospel. No one in our mission had ever hit that number, but we wanted to push barriers, and we believed that God would bless us for our hard work.

It was the last day of the week, and we had already reached our goal of fifty phone numbers. We were on the bus home and began calling through the phone numbers we had received to see when we could meet with these people again. As we called, however, person after person told us they were "too busy" or just didn't pick up. Not a single person we called seemed to be interested or willing to make the time to meet with us. We were crushed. Had our hard work been in vain? Had we become too number-oriented?

With these thoughts swirling around in my head, I decided to strike up a conversation with the person sitting next to me on the bus. As soon as I did, a lady on the row in front of us leaned back and asked my companion, "Are you guys Christian?"

Although we never again met a single one of the fifty people we got phone numbers from, the lady on the bus was baptized three months later.

It wasn't that the other fifty people were a waste of our time, but rather that God knew who was prepared, and once we gave our full effort, He blessed us. By sincerely talking with everyone and working hard, you will not only gain God's trust but also His friends.

NO EFFORT IS WASTED

MATTHEW

"We should bring Bryan with us," I said to Elder York. Elder York and I had been companions for almost three months, and we had been working with an eighteen-year-old named Bryan who was preparing for a mission. We had gotten him a bike, and he started to accompany us for a few hours a day because he had recently finished school. With an hour between two of our appointments, we decided it was a good time to have Bryan try talking to strangers with us. We prayed, felt impressed to go in a certain direction, and began talking to anyone we could find who would listen to us.

Eventually we came to a neighborhood near our next appointment and began knocking on several doors. A few houses in, we heard Bryan say out of the blue, "David?"

There, in one of the doorways, was another young eighteen-year-old. "Oh, hey, Bryan! What are you doing around here?"

"Well, I'm actually out here with my missionary friends looking for people who are interested in learning about Jesus Christ," Bryan replied.

To our astonishment, David said, "Well, my dad is Buddhist, and my mom is Muslim, but I am neither. I've always wanted to learn about Jesus Christ."

Seizing the opportunity, we began teaching David. For two weeks, we taught David, and he even came to church. Then, out of nowhere, he disappeared. None of us could get in touch with him, and no matter how many times we stopped by his house, no one was ever home.

I soon left the area and figured David was gone forever. I served the rest of my mission and honestly forgot all about David until the week after I arrived home to Utah and received a message request on Facebook. It was David! Then came the shocking part. In his profile photo, David was standing all dressed in white with the missionaries. He had been baptized the week before. In his message David said to me, "Thanks for being the first to find me. I was baptized last week, Elder Spurrier!" He went on to explain how life circumstances had taken him away from the opportunity to learn while I was serving in his area. When his circumstances had changed, he found Bryan and the missionaries and continued his learning. David left for his mission in December 2019, and now he, too, is planting seeds in God's kingdom.

You never know how you will affect the people you talk to on the street or teach just one or two lessons to. Talking with everyone allows people to use their agency and exercise faith. Then, even if you're rejected, you can be confident that some of the seeds you planted will one day blossom under the right circumstances.

On our missions, we taught the exact principles and techniques discussed throughout this chapter in district meetings, zone meetings, and mission leadership councils. Hundreds of missionaries have offered testimonials of their effectiveness. We have included just one for motivation:

> Oh [they] were right. These last few days I've been doing all I can to talk to people. And I've gotten [my companion] in on it. Our numbers from last week exploded. We got more [contacts] than the last three weeks together, I think. It was only twelve, but they are SOLID. We achieved and for the most part exceeded our goals. We are happy. We've prayed with about four people in the last few days and most of them were near tears. We stop some of the most prepared people. I've been feeling the Spirit more. I am bolder. I feel that I can be a positive change for good. I even EAT healthier because I feel more empowered. Bad things just don't seem good anymore. Our time is spent more meaningfully.

Studies have been better. Focus has been there. I've had some interesting dreams. Our branch president trusts us. We have miracle lessons and less active members coming out of the woodwork. (Sister Sow)

CHALLENGE #6
INVITE SOMEONE TO BE BAPTIZED OVER PIZZA
—OR—
HAVE A CONVERSATION WITH THREE STRANGERS
PLEASE CHOOSE AND COMMIT TO ONE OF THE ABOVE

HELPFUL SUGGESTIONS

- See if you can find out two interesting facts about each of these strangers.

- See if you can determine one problem that each of these strangers is working through, or one righteous desire they might have.

- Study the following sections from *Preach My Gospel,* chapter nine:
  "Talking with Everyone" (page 156).
  "Teach When You Find, Find When You Teach" (page 158).
  "Developing the Faith to Find" (page 155).

CHAPTER 7
SET GOALS, MAKE PLANS

I am so thoroughly convinced that if we don't [learn to] set goals [and make plans] . . . we can . . . look back on our life only to see that we reached but a small part of our full potential.

—Elder M. Russell Ballard (*Preach My Gospel*, 146)

WHAT MAKES A S.M.A.R.T. GOAL?

When you set goals, set S.M.A.R.T. goals. They should be

SPECIFIC (Would someone else be able to understand your goal?)

MEASUREABLE (How will you track your progress?)

ACHIEVABLE (Do you believe you can reach your goal?)

RELEVANT (Does hitting your goal include someone becoming more Christlike?)

TIME-BOUND (How long do you have to complete your goal?)

On your mission, you will want to set goals each day, each week, each transfer, and for your entire mission. Setting S.M.A.R.T. goals will make seemingly impossible goals possible.

MATTHEW

Near the end of my mission, I wasn't even in the same galaxy to reach some of the ridiculous goals I had set when I started my mission. With six months left to serve, I still wanted to become more Christlike, get better at the Malay language, read more scriptures, try new foods, and help more people come unto Christ. The last goal seemed the most overwhelming: be a part of eleven more baptisms. Although I felt it was near impossible, I decided to have faith that "I can do all things through Christ who strengtheneth me" (Philippians 4:13). I took out the original goals I had set on the first day of my mission and broke down every main goal into smaller S.M.A.R.T. goals, coupled with specific plans.

Matthew's rewritten goal sheet

This sheet was taped into the back of my daily planner for the rest of my mission (so I had to see it every day). I worked on the goals every single day, and through the blessings of God, I managed to achieve every single one of them. On the last day of my mission, I was even blessed with the opportunity to baptize one of the people we were teaching and achieve my goal of being a part of exactly eleven more baptisms. This was not a coincidence. God honors our desires, which manifest themselves through the S.M.A.R.T. goals we sincerely set with Him.

WHAT'S *NOT* A S.M.A.R.T. GOAL?

It's common to set a goal and then look back later to realize no progress has been made. We've all done it. In this section, we've detailed common mistakes that missionaries make when setting goals.

In our experience, one of the most common missionary goals is "to have more charity." Based on the S.M.A.R.T. methodology that we just shared, unless broken down into smaller, more specific goals coupled with plans, this is an abstract goal that can't be targeted. Charity is the most important attribute any person can develop, and we aren't disagreeing with Mormon or Paul when they wrote that "if ye have not charity, ye are nothing." However, that doesn't mean setting a goal "to have more charity" is the right way to obtain this priceless Christlike attribute (Mormon 7:46; 1 Corinthians 13:2). Instead, try starting out a bit more specific. For example, you could set a goal to pray daily for the gift of charity, or to do one random act of service each day for your companion.

Another common mistake missionaries make is to set a goal of zero. For example, some missionaries may say, "Oh well, today we don't have any lessons planned with any new people so we will set a goal of zero new people taught today." Don't do it! Zero is *not* a goal, and it never will be. Zero can't be a goal, because there is no "faith in the Lord Jesus Christ" in zero. A goal of zero is generally just an expectation that is derived from past experiences. When our desires are combined with faith in Christ, the results are always bigger than our own efforts—therefore they are always greater than zero. If you don't have any lessons planned, then set a goal of one on faith and make plans to call through past contacts to set up a lesson with someone new. "Meaningful goals and careful planning will help you accomplish what the Lord requires of you" (*Preach My Gospel*, 137).

MATTHEW

In my first area, we consistently set a goal of zero people we were teaching attending church. Quite honestly, I didn't believe that we could really get anyone to come to church. Our focus was to exceed our goals, which, for us, meant setting low goals and being surprised if we beat them. However, this mindset had us slipping into complacency.

One week, we set a goal of zero people with a baptismal date and zero people attending church. Can you guess what happened? To no surprise, we ended the week with zero people with a baptismal date and zero people attending church. I remember thinking, "Why not shoot for the stars with our goals? At least we would be trying!" So that's exactly what we did.

My companion and I had recently found a new family of nine to teach, so we prayed and decided that this would be the week they would come to church. We set our goal: nine people attending church.

At first, I had no idea how they could all attend, because they lived forty-five minutes away from the church building and only owned two small mopeds, but we decided to have faith that through Christ, it was possible. Our zone leaders called us and asked, "Are you sure you don't want to set a lower goal? You had zero last week, so maybe a goal of one or two is better." They might have had a point, but we had set our goal with God and didn't budge. We were going to find a way to get all nine family members to church.

That week we taught them about the Restoration three times in three different ways, all focused on how one can know the fruits of the gospel by going to church. After hitting home the doctrine of why they should attend church, we then explained our plan for how to get them there, despite their inconvenient circumstances. We arranged to have a branch member give two of them a ride, three of them would ride the bus, and the other four could ride their two mopeds. That Sunday, not only did all nine of them attend church, but we also had two additional men come that we had found by talking with everyone. The zone leaders were shocked.

That day I learned three things: First, never underestimate the how of your goals. Spend sufficient time working out the logistics. Second, although we should set attainable goals, never allow attainability to transform into complacency. And third, "You get what you go for," because, through God, all things are possible if it be His will (Boyd K. Packer, as quoted in the commencement remarks of Elder Don R. Clarke at BYU–Idaho, July 20, 2012; thechurchnews.com/archives/2012-07-27/byu-idaho-a-bountiful-harvest-50603).

Matthew and his companion with the family of nine

WHEN YOU DON'T HIT YOUR GOALS

Sometimes you might have the smartest goals, you might be the best missionary there ever was, and you still might not hit your goal.

DAKOTA AND MATTHEW

Matthew and I became companions in a Filipino ward (despite speaking Malay and Chinese) and, at the time, we honestly believed we would baptize every single Filipino and Filipina that walked the country of Singapore. At first, we had many people to teach, and some on date for baptism. With a running start, we set lofty goals, because we thought it was the will of the Lord. The weeks came and went, and all the people we taught went with them. Each week we would have, on average, eight people we were teaching attend church, and yet no one was progressing. Every week it seemed, our eight people attending church would be eight different people.

After three months full of a bunch of "numbers" and no real success, Dakota and I were confused. We sat down with our mission president and asked him, "Where have we gone wrong? Nothing seems to be working."

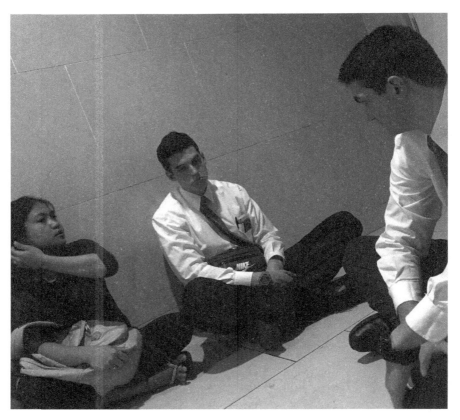

Matthew and Dakota, saddened at yet another person's inability to keep commitments

He told us, "Perhaps you are doing everything right, but there's something greater God needs you to learn through this trial."

Dakota and I were lucky enough to stay together for a third transfer. This go-around, we took the time to redo all our goals and humble ourselves before the Lord. We realized that perhaps we hadn't relied on Him enough the first time. This time we would simply enjoy the work, do what we knew was right, and find His will in the numerical goals we set that represented His children in Singapore. We decided to set a more realistic goal of three baptisms for that transfer. Six weeks later, on our last Sunday together, three people we had been teaching were baptized. God instructed us over those five months that He cared more about who we were becoming than success in numbers. We learned by experience that He had His own timing but still cared about our righteous goals.

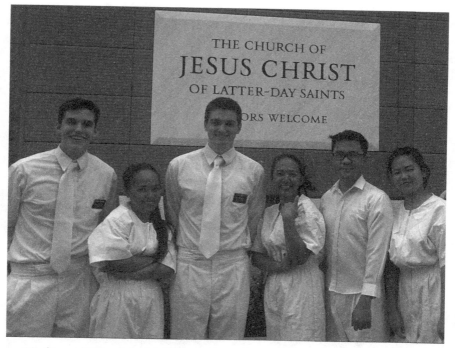

Matthew and Dakota's final day as companions when they were finally able to see their work come to fruition with three baptisms

Our story here has a happy-ever-after ending, but since then, we've often wondered what would have happened if things didn't work out. What if we had re-evaluated our goals, prayed to include the Lord, and still nothing had worked out for us? What then?

During these far-from-picture-perfect moments that we all have, it helps to remember to protect your *priorities* from your *goals*.

For example, in missionary work, you will have goals to baptize people—and you should. Jesus commanded us to make that a goal (Matthew 28:19). However, baptizing is not our priority. Love for God and our fellow man is our priority (see Matthew 12:30–31).

If someone you are teaching ever tells you, like they have told us, "I will try to come to church so that you guys can hit your quota," you'll know that you've lost sight of your priorities within your goals. We must learn to be the master of our goals, not the servant. Goals are not the boss. They are tools—tools that when aligned with the will of the Father in prayer will enable you to accomplish more than you could have ever imagined, perhaps in ways you didn't imagine.

DAKOTA

During my time in college at MIT, my goal was to have a perfect GPA. However, as time went on, and with college basketball and a commitment to my fraternity weighing on my already limited time, I began to slowly copy more and more of the hardest homework problems. At the time, it seemed like no big deal, because these homework problems covered material that wasn't on the tests.

It wasn't until my senior year that my dishonest conduct finally became clear to me. After copying the hardest part of a homework assignment, I received an email from my professor stating that I had received a "zero" for the entire assignment due to my blatant copying.

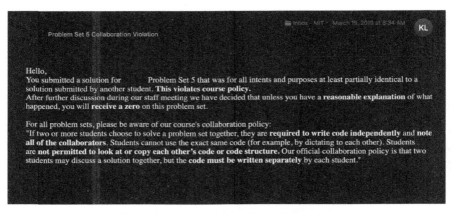

The original email from the teaching staff regarding Dakota's cheating

Out of guilt, I immediately decided to apologize to all my professors in whose classes I had copied certain homework problems. Before I did so, I had the thought to pray. As I spoke with my Heavenly Father, I had the distinct impression that by first apologizing to my professors, I would be committing the same sin. By apologizing first to my professors, I would be putting my professors above God and setting my goals above my priorities.

Finally understanding my fundamental flaw, I decided to first apologize to God. I had let my goal to have good grades take precedence over my priority to love God by being completely honest in all facets of my life. In the end, I never reached my goal to have a perfect GPA, but the lesson I learned was so much more meaningful.

When we honor our priorities, not hitting any or all goals becomes less disturbing. When we honor our priorities we can have confidence and hope in Christ and His redeeming power, which is more important than hitting any goal you could ever set. "The ultimate measure of success is not in achieving goals alone but in the service you render and the progress of others" *(Preach My Gospel*, 146).

NEVER SET A GOAL WITHOUT A PLAN

Just as important as understanding how to set goals is learning how to make effective plans in order to reach your goals. At the beginning of our missions, we figured it was easier to make plans and then set goals to match those plans, but that ruins the point of a goal in the first place. A goal is supposed to push you, not match what you are already going to accomplish without it.

Preach My Gospel chapter eight states over and over again, "Set goals and [then] make plans." The act of praying to God and then setting goals for the following day, week, or transfer with your companion is putting your faith in Jesus Christ first. Once you have decided on some faith-filled goals, then you can go through your next day, week, or transfer and make plans for you, your companion, and the Holy Ghost to achieve those goals.

Generally, one single daily plan won't do the job, since original plans can often fall through or change. You need to make a primary plan followed by a backup plan, and then more backup plans for your backup plan. Anyone who has served a mission will tell you that 99 percent of your time on your mission doesn't go as planned. This is usually because although you may have a good plan, God has a better one, and He wants to see if you have the faith to follow it.

Let's consider Nephi, for example. Nephi and his brothers had one goal from the Lord: to obtain the brass plates from Laban. Once they set their goal, they knew where to put their energy. First, they tried simply talking with Laban. After that didn't work, Laman and Lemuel (you might have a Laman or Lemuel as a companion) decided it was time to quit, but Nephi said, "As the Lord liveth, and as we live, we will not go down unto our father in the wilderness until we have accomplished the thing which the Lord hath commanded us" (1 Nephi 3:15). For you, that might mean dipping into your lunch or dinnertime to hit the goal you set with God. Or, that might mean actually having and using your backup plan. Nephi's backup plan was to gather their "gold and silver and precious things" and do a swap for the brass plates with Laban (1 Nephi 3:22). Once again, not successful.

At this point we'd guess Nephi had the same thoughts that we had many times on our missions: "Okay God, I set this goal with you. How in the world am I going to complete it?" Nephi could have sat in the wilderness and thought, "Well, I tried my best, so now I'll just wait for God to do His part." But he didn't wait in the wilderness. He didn't expect God to bring the brass plates out to him on a golden platter. Nephi thought, "God, I have tried everything I know how to, but this is our goal, and so I will go back once more even though I don't really know how this is going to work." Nephi "was led by the Spirit, not knowing beforehand the things which [he] should do" (1 Nephi 4:6). And as you know, God took care of the rest.

God created the entire universe. How easy would it have been for Him to bring out the brass plates to Nephi on a golden platter in the wilderness? Just a snap of his fingers, and boom—done. But He didn't. Why not? Because God expects us to show faith, past what we sometimes feel is reasonable. He needs us to stretch. That is what we are here on earth to do. "The good works that really matter require the help of heaven. And the help of heaven requires working past the point of fatigue so far that only the meek and lowly will keep going long enough. The Lord doesn't put us through this test just to give us a grade; he does it because the process will change us" (Henry B. Eyring, "Waiting upon the Lord," fireside address, Brigham Young University, Sept. 30, 1990).

MIRACLES HAVE NOT CEASED

You might be thinking, "Nephi and his brothers are part of the scriptures. Things don't happen like that today." This is completely false (see Mormon 9:15–21).

MATTHEW AND DAKOTA

It was a Monday night, and we had set up a family home evening with a member to help them invite their friends to learn about the restored gospel (plan 1), but that fell through. Typical.

"Well," we decided, "we don't have time for dinner because of meetings, but we could eat dinner with a stranger and ask them to learn the gospel" (plan 2). So we ate dinner, but no one else eating seemed to be interested in talking with us. Thirty minutes later, we still didn't have anything to do.

In our daily planner, our backup plan said, "Walk through the Botanic Gardens." We looked up at each other and laughed. "Why did we write that down?" we asked each other.

The Singapore Botanic Gardens was more of a tourist spot, somewhere missionaries would typically go to relax on a preparation day, not to actually find people to teach. Even though it seemed like a waste of our time, we both had the spiritual impression to go anyway. We prayed and said something along the lines of "God, we don't know why we are going here, but we will go anyway." Just like Nephi, we "not knowing beforehand the things which [we] should do," began walking through the Botanic Gardens, looking for a Filipino to talk to since we were serving in the Filipino ward at the time (1 Nephi 4:6). As we entered the gardens, we stopped and took a selfie with a quaint little gazebo behind us.

The selfie photo in the Botanic Gardens with the gazebo, circled

A minute later, we walked into the gazebo, and, to our astonishment, a Filipino woman was sitting inside reading her Bible. *What in the world!* we thought. Seizing the opportunity, we sat down and began reading the Bible with her. Six weeks later, she was baptized. To this day, we are grateful that we were brave enough to follow God's plan and not ours, even when we did not understand why we were supposed to.

KEY PLANNING PRINCIPLES

We will leave the specifics for how to plan up to you, but we are going to give you a few pointers.

- To start, it's useful to use a shortened version of the thirteen steps outlined in *Preach My Gospel* chapter eight for "The Weekly Planning Session" in your daily planning sessions.

- You should keep detailed descriptions of people's lesson topics and commitments. This serves two purposes: first, you'll remember what you committed them to do and what you have taught them before, and second, if new missionaries come into the area, they can read what you've written in order to pick up where you left off.

- You should plan throughout the current day for the next day. This means setting up appointments for the next day throughout the current day. Planning time is not the time to answer the phone or call people to set up appointments, but rather a spiritual meeting with the Holy Ghost to discern the needs of the people you teach and those in your area.

- Take thirty seconds at the end of your daily planning session to make sure both you and your companion are in sync. Ask your companion, "Are we united right now? Is there anything bothering you? If so, let's talk about it."

- Scheduling is generally the last step of planning. Planning first includes the discussion of an individual's needs, not the scheduling of your lunch break. If you find yourself starting your planning session off by going through the day's activities and appointments, you've missed the whole point. It's about the people first! What do they need? How can you help them?

The following is an example of what a daily planner should and should not look like after a planning session. Can you guess which is which? What details stick out to you about the good planner versus the bad planner? Whether you use a paper or digital planner, the principles are the same. This is how our planners really looked at the beginning of our missions and then later near the end of our missions. A good planning session makes the day stress free! "You can tell how effective your daily plans are when you don't need to ask others, 'Now what should I do?'" (*Preach My Gospel*, 150).

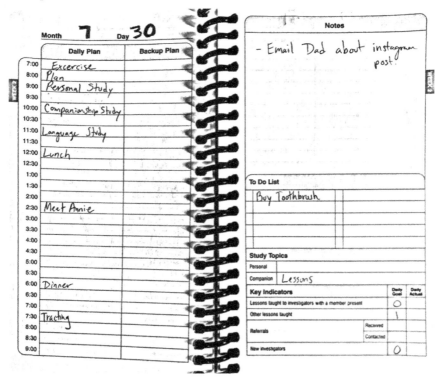

An example of a daily plan near the beginning of Dakota's and Matthew's missions

An example of a daily plan near the end of Dakota's and Matthew's missions

FULL-PURPOSE MISSIONARIES

Preach My Gospel teaches, "Have a meaningful activity planned for every hour of the day" (page 150). We're going to take the liberty to ask you to "have a [different] activity planned for every hour of the day" if possible. Full-purpose missionaries are missionaries who are able to find, teach, baptize, reactivate, and retain every day. Full-purpose plans allow missionaries to do that. So how do you plan with full purpose?

For example, let's say you have three hours of free time in an afternoon. Rather than just going to the town square and handing out pamphlets for three straight hours (boring!), we would encourage you to visit a less active member in town and talk to everyone on the way there and back. There are multiple reasons for this.

First, you are getting two things done at once. You are finding new people to teach at the same time you are attempting to reactivate less active members who have strayed from the fold. There are almost always more than enough less active members, active members, and past people taught or contacted to visit so that you will never have to just go hand out pamphlets for three hours.

Second, it gives you a place to go. We've found that when you have a destination in mind, rather than just standing in the town square or knocking random doors on a street, people tend to be more receptive.

Tracting is probably the most common plan among missionaries worldwide. However, it's usually not the most effective. Tracting can be defined as picking a neighborhood or apartment complex and then knocking every single door as a way to find new people to teach. This strategy can be successful, and, by all means, if the Spirit prompts you to tract, then please listen. However, in our experience, tracting isn't very fun.

Going tracting for extended periods of time often destroys your energy and attitude. Mixing up your plans, on the other hand, keeps your life interesting and balanced and your attitude positive. When your energy and attitude are positive, your success rate explodes. Remember, "Attitude is [still] everything." That's not going to change, no matter what chapter we are in.

MATTHEW

Elder Bradley and I were both brand new to our area. We didn't know anything or anyone. We had planned to visit a few people our first day, but other than that, we didn't have much going for us yet.

It would have been easy to say, "Let's go tracting from 1:00–3:00 p.m.," because there were plenty of new neighborhoods and busy markets we could have gone to. Instead, we decided to pray and then choose who we could pay a visit to while talking to people along the way.

"Sister Joy!" Elder Bradley said.

"Woah, where did that come from?" I asked.

"Her name is the first one on the ward list!" exclaimed Elder Bradley. We looked at each other and laughed. (Sometimes revelation can be as simple as that.)

We left the house with purpose in our hearts and a prayer of faith. Along the way, we sang to people on the train, prayed with people in the streets, handed out pamphlets, and even invited someone to be baptized if they came to know what we shared was true.

Finally arriving at Sister Joy's house after over an hour of walking and talking to people, we knocked on her door. To our surprise, a grumpy old Chinese man opened the door.

"I don't speak English," the man said as he began to close the door in our faces.

"How is your day?" asked Elder Bradley in Chinese, putting his hand on the door. The old grandpa's jaw dropped. He was clearly stunned to hear a white kid speak Chinese. "Is Sister Joy here?" Elder Bradley continued in Chinese.

"She doesn't live here," the old man answered.

All of a sudden, a little boy ran up and said, "Hey, that's my mom's name!" The Chinese uncle looked at us awkwardly and slowly inched away from the doorway.

"Your mom is Joy?" I asked the little boy. Indeed she was. We took out a plan of salvation pamphlet and wrote on the back, "Just as this pamphlet teaches, God has a plan for each of us, and we know He has a plan for you, Sister Joy. God sent us to your house today to help you find the peace and joy you have been looking for again in your life." We handed it to the little boy and left.

That night, we received a call from Sister Joy. She asked us if she could come to church with us. (She was a bit nervous because it had been a long time since she had last been there.) That Sunday, she came to church, and she didn't miss a single week the entire three months I served in that ward. Soon after, her son was baptized, she became the ward Gospel Principles teacher, and to this day, she is one of the best member missionaries in the entire country of Singapore.

Sister Joy, pictured center, at her son's baptism

That day, Elder Bradley and I were full-purpose missionaries. We talked with people on the way to Sister Joy's house (finding many potential contacts), helped reactivate a depressed Sister Joy, and eventually baptized her son. What more could you ask for? God's work can be as simple as that, but it all starts with a full-purpose plan.

God didn't put us on earth for any random reason. His goal to "bring to pass the immortality and eternal life of man" wasn't some abstract goal (Moses 1:39). As the author of His plan of salvation, He made detailed plans for His billions and billions of children. You are one of those children. The sad part is that many of God's detailed plans will fall through and never happen. We've often asked ourselves why God still set those goals and made those plans, knowing that many of us would fall off the path and never reach eternal life. But we've come to realize that not making the effort means accepting the status quo, unfairness, wasted potential, and complacency, and that's not the person God would ever allow Himself to be. Yes, many of God's plans for us will fall through. However, that doesn't make God any less perfect. Perfection is not measured by hitting every single goal or following through with every single plan. God's perfection is His absolute consecration, regardless of His children's responses to His efforts. Our progression toward perfection will be achieved in the same way. "Practice doesn't make perfect. Christ makes perfect" (see Brad Wilcox, *Changed through His Grace*). So let us strive to set goals and make plans with Him.

CHALLENGE #7

SUCCESSFULLY ANSWER THE QUESTIONS BELOW BY SETTING GOALS AND MAKING PLANS

Take a few minutes and think about your final day in the mission field. When that day comes

1. What do you want to say you have done as a missionary?

2. Who do you want to have become?

3. What differences would you want others (or yourself) to notice in you?

4. How are you going to accomplish these goals?
   (See *Preach My Gospel*, 152.)

HELPFUL SUGGESTIONS

Here are some goal ideas, followed by some suggested plans to help you accomplish them:

- Gain a stronger relationship with God.

  * What books of scripture you want to read, and how many times you want to read them.

  * Pray for five minutes every day.

  * Pray daily for a specific gift of the Spirit that you'd like to develop.

  * Repent every day.

- Become fluent in your mission language.

  * Speak only your mission language to your companion (whether your companion is native or not).

  * Memorize ten new vocabulary words every day.

  * Write down five new words you hear each day.

- Develop Charity.
  - * Do one small act of service for your companion or family member each day.
  - * Pray for the gift of charity each day.

- Baptize (list a certain number) of people.
  - * Give out (a certain number) of copies of the Book of Mormon.
  - * Talk to (a certain number) of people each week, each transfer, etc.

- Reactivate (a certain number) of people.
  - * Visit (a certain number) of less active members each week.
  - * Pray each week to know which less active members to focus on.

ALTERNATE CHALLENGES

- Plan an activity and invite people to attend (family, a date, friends, etc.). Help them participate. If possible, plan it with another person.
- Record (in your phone or physical planner) all the events you have for a week. Review or modify those plans each day. Evaluate your progress at the end of the week. Report to someone you trust.

CHAPTER 8
THE MASTER TEACHER

You will most likely teach thousands of lessons on your mission (whether on the streets or in homes), but teaching a lot of lessons doesn't guarantee that you'll become a master teacher. The Pharisees and the Sadducees had lots of practice going to church and learning and teaching about the prophesied Messiah, but they still failed to recognize the Son of God in the flesh. With this is mind, it's clear that practice doesn't make perfect, but rather, practice makes permanent.

When the apostles and prophets wrote *Preach My Gospel*, they did so with one scripture in mind:

> Neither take ye thought beforehand what ye shall say; but treasure up in your minds continually the words of life, and it shall be given you in the very hour that portion that shall be meted unto every man. (D&C 84:85)

The Apostles wanted to write *Preach My Gospel* in such a way that you could not memorize the lessons but rather the concepts (Elder Brent H. Nielson, fireside, 2015). Succinctly put, God is not in the business of completing lessons but in completing people.

PREPARING LESSON PLANS—THE CIBID SEQUENCE

Just because the Apostles don't want you to memorize your lessons doesn't mean you shouldn't prepare one. To plan your lesson, first think about the person's individual needs, and then try going through the CIBID SEQuence. (The CIBID SEQuence is an acronym based on *Preach My Gospel*'s instruction for planning lessons. See "Studying and Preparing to Teach the Lessons," 19–21.) It helps remind us what the Apostles advise us to do when we are preparing for a lesson. It goes like this:

COMMITMENT INVITATION—What do you want each person you are teaching to do between now and your next lesson? This is the most critical part, because the rest of the lesson plan should all be pointed toward helping them keep this commitment. (The scriptures, examples, and everything else you share in your lesson should support the invitation you plan to extend.)

BAPTISMAL INVITATION—As the Spirit directs, invite those you teach to come unto Christ through baptism. Think about the baptismal interview questions and how what you are teaching can point your listeners toward preparing to answer them.

DOCTRINE—What doctrine have you prepared to teach them?

SCRIPTURES—Have you prepared specific scriptures to share?

EXAMPLES—Have you prepared examples to illustrate the doctrine from the scriptures or from your family, friends, or your life? Don't be afraid to share personal experiences. In fact, we've found that sharing personal experiences helps create unique emotional bonds. You are not a robot missionary. You are you for a reason. Be you.

QUESTIONS—Have you prepared one or two well-thought-out questions? A good question is a game changer and can make the difference between helping someone find Christ and losing their interest.

DAKOTA AND MATTHEW

Matthew and I were teaching a man named Sam from Myanmar who was living in Singapore at the time. His English was subpar, to say the least. Although he seemed interested in the gospel, we could tell our lessons with him weren't going very well. It felt like we were force-feeding an elephant to a mouse. We prepared each lesson using the CIBID SEQuence, but they still felt forced, and they were clearly difficult for him to understand.

One day before his lesson, we prayed to God asking for help in understanding how we could really connect with Sam. What personal experience did we need to share? What insightful question did we need to ask? Perhaps we needed the Burmese gift of tongues?

That day's lesson started no differently from the others. We were teaching the Word of Wisdom, but twenty minutes into the lesson, I suddenly felt prompted to ask a question we had not prepared to ask—a question far off the topic at hand.

"Sam, what . . . you . . . like . . . about . . . church?" I asked in my simplest English.

He looked at me and smiled. With emotion filling his face, he responded, "My family—forever."

Matthew and I looked at each other. Never once had we mentioned eternal families to Sam. We didn't even know he knew the concept existed. Nonetheless, Sam had just testified of one of the great truths of the gospel, that families can be together forever.

From then on, Matthew and I did our best to connect every lesson and piece of the gospel back to eternal families. Sam loved it. Our lessons went better than ever, and he was baptized a month later. Had we not taken the time to find out what was important to Sam, I'm afraid our force-fed lessons may have turned him off from joining the Church. Remember, using the CIBID SEQuence shows God you are striving to be His dedicated servant, but spiritual promptings trump all. Have the courage to change your plans mid-lesson according to the Spirit. It's more important for people to learn than for you to teach. Give those you teach adequate time to talk. Their "witness of the Holy Ghost should be the central focus of your teaching" (*Preach My Gospel*, 103).

Two years later, Sam and his fiancée were sealed for time and all eternity in the Manila Philippines Temple. His dream of having an eternal family is coming true.

Sam and his wife, married in the Manila Philippines Temple, December 18, 2018

REVIEWING LESSON PLANS

The Apostles advise us not only to plan each lesson beforehand but to also review each lesson afterward. With your companion, practice using the ABCDEFFG acronym to review each lesson, learning from what you did and did not do well (see *Preach My Gospel*, 21).

ASK QUESTIONS—Did you ask thoughtful questions? Did you listen with real intent?

BAPTISM—Did you mention baptism? Did you refer to at least one of the baptismal interview questions?

COMMITMENT—Did you give them a specific commitment? Make sure to write it down so you don't forget and can follow up later.

DOCTRINE—Did you cover applicable doctrine?

EXPRESS TESTIMONY—Did you bear testimony with power and authority?

FRIENDS—Did you ask them to refer their friends?

FOLLOW UP—Did you follow up on the commitment from last lesson?

GHOST—Was the Spirit present in your lesson? Why or why not?

Using the ABCDEFFG acronym to review takes one to two minutes after each lesson and quickly identifies your teaching strengths and weaknesses.

SETTING EXPECTATIONS

MATTHEW

When I started my mission, my mom loved the idea that strangers were letting me into their homes to share with them my testimony of Jesus Christ. One day, while I was on my mission, a pair of Jehovah's Witness missionaries stopped at our home in Utah. Thinking of me, my mom let them in to share a message.

She figured that if Singaporeans and Malaysians were willing to hear me out, she should be willing to listen to other types of missionaries.

After that first visit, the Jehovah's Witness missionaries came to our home several more times and shared comfortable, uplifting messages. After several meetings, they finally asked my mom why she was meeting with them and if she was interested in coming to their church. My mom then explained, "My son is on a mission for The Church of Jesus Christ of Latter-day Saints, so I figured I should be kind and hear you out. I'm strong in my faith but think highly of you two and the nice messages you share." As you might guess, after that day, the Jehovah's Witness missionaries never came back to our home again.

Now, you might think this could never happen to you. You might think you will always make sure that the people you teach are sincere in their learning. I thought the same thing, but I couldn't tell you how many times this happened to me. In the first lesson, people need to know the purpose of your visits. When the people you teach aren't willing to be baptized if they come to know the truth of the gospel, as hard as it may be, you should seriously consider moving on. Follow the Spirit always, but sometimes you just need to plant the seed. You can always check back on them in a few weeks or months. You, as well as they, will be better off if you have the faith to do that (see *Preach My Gospel*, "How to Begin Teaching," 176).

HOW LONG SHOULD YOUR LESSONS BE?

Missionaries sometimes believe that by spending hours and hours at a member's house you will "develop a good relationship" with them. That might work sometimes, but "hanging out" is definitely not an effective method of missionary work. You can leave a better impression from a thirty-minute meeting than a four-hour hangout.

Think about Super Bowl commercials. These are the best commercials made, and they only last an average of thirty seconds. We should always leave them wanting more. As missionaries, we want to hit them with the Spirit and then leave. As you leave, they will feel the Spirit leave with you and wonder, "Where did that good feeling go so quickly?" They will want you to come back, because you didn't take up their entire afternoon explaining the deep meaning of Kolob or playing darts with their children. There is a time and place for those things outside of missionary life. The Spirit's impression upon the soul is so much more lasting and effective than anything else. *Preach My Gospel* teaches that "rarely should a lesson go over 45 minutes" (vii, 72). However, in our experience, if you are going to rarely have lessons that go over forty-five minutes, you need to aim for lessons of thirty minutes or less.

THE FIRST VISION

I saw a pillar of light exactly over my head, above the brightness of the sun, which descended gradually until it fell upon me.

. . . When the light rested upon me I saw two Personages, whose brightness and glory defy all description, standing above me in the air. One of them spake unto me, calling me by name and said, pointing to the other—*This is My Beloved Son. Hear Him!* (Joseph Smith's account of the First Vision, Joseph Smith—History 1:16–17)

MATTHEW

To this day, every time I say the First Vision out loud, I can feel the Holy Ghost pumping through my body. Repeating Joseph Smith's personal account of the First Vision is one of the most powerful tools to bring the Spirit into a lesson. Everything that the Church, you, and I stand for hinges on that single moment, because it proves to the world that God still cares. Mormon asks, "And if there were miracles wrought [during Christ's time], why has God ceased to be a God of miracles?" Then, answering his own question (a good teaching technique in and of itself), Mormon responds, "And behold, I say unto you he changeth not; if so he would cease to be God; and he ceaseth not to be God, and is a God of miracles" (Mormon 9:19). The First Vision proves that God doesn't change and that just as He called prophets of old to warn people of sin and testify of Christ, He calls prophets today.

Matthew relating the First Vision on the streets of Malaysia

108

As you relate Joseph Smith's First Vision to the people you teach, take your time to use his exact wording. I would suggest memorizing it in English and your mission language while you are in the MTC. Once you can state the First Vision forward and backward, it's easier to focus on the Spirit around the event rather than worrying about forgetting the words. I said it every morning when I woke up, just to make sure I never forgot it. I testify you will see many tears of joy (whether they be your own or the people you teach) as you relate the First Vision with real intent.

MATTHEW

Once, I was training a new missionary named Elder Hackett, and we were practicing the First Vision in Malay. As he role-played it with me, he repeated it very quickly, but I stopped him.

"Elder Hackett," I said, "let me relate how this should be shared in my opinion." I began giving some background on Joseph Smith and his soul-searching questions. Then I looked Elder Hackett right in the eyes and began slowly saying the First Vision to him. I really put my heart into it. I wanted him to not only understand what happened but also feel what happened. Tears welled up in his eyes. He couldn't have fully understood what I said, because he was new to the mission language, but he could feel in his heart the truth of Joseph Smith's words. He had heard the First Vision hundreds of times, but as I slowly went through it and really meant what I said, the Spirit pricked his heart. "Wow!" Elder Hackett gleefully said. "That must be true!"

"The Savior is the master teacher. Jesus has been described as a philosopher, an economist, a social reformer, and many other things. But more than these, the Savior was a teacher. If you were to ask, 'What did Jesus have as an occupation?' There is only one answer: He was a teacher . . . the master teacher" (Boyd K. Packer, *Mine Errand from the Lord*). If you read the scriptures with an eye for teaching skills, you will find all the principles we've shared in this chapter and more. Christ promises that "by the weak things . . . [He] shall thresh the nations" (D&C 133:59). Is it a coincidence that eighteen- and seventy-year-olds are generally the ones called to preach the gospel as full-time missionaries? Are we not "the weak?" Certainly there are stronger members of the Church.

For now, you can use this chapter as a cheat sheet, but remember, practice doesn't necessarily make perfect. Following Jesus Christ does. If we let Him, Christ will create master teachers of each of us.

CHALLENGE #8

PLAN A LESSON WITH THE MISSIONARIES AND THEN HELP TEACH THAT LESSON

HELPFUL SUGGESTIONS

- Use the CIBID SEQuence to plan and the ABCDEFFG to review when you help the missionaries teach.
- Memorize the First Vision.
- Read 3 Nephi 11–18 and think about how Jesus Christ focused on people while still sticking to the central purpose for His visit.

CHAPTER 9
MEMBERS MAKE MIRACLES

The ideal situation is when members invite others to
be taught and are present for the teaching. When
members do this, more people are baptized and remain
active in the Church. —*Preach My Gospel*, 160

MEMBERS BRIDGE THE GAP

The best missionary work is done when members know the person who is being
taught or develop a friendship with them. Compared with missionaries, members tend to have a better understanding of common cultural concerns and reside
in the local area for longer periods of time. Given these advantages, we've found
that sometimes people will even tell members their concerns about what you're
teaching before they tell you. As much as you may try to be normal, you are still
this weird "church employee" who might not be native to the country, probably
isn't completely fluent in the local language, seemingly doesn't fully understand the
culture, and has to follow a bunch of strict rules.

DAKOTA

I was nearing the end of my mission, and in my mind, I had mastered the
Chinese language and missionary work as a whole. If there was a master missionary, I thought I was it. I could do anything and baptize anyone. I was very wrong.

Around that time, my companion and I began teaching a young woman named Feng from Sichuan, China. At first, she progressed quickly, and we had even given her a baptismal date, but then she began to struggle with serious doubts and questions. Owing to my overconfidence, I had slacked on inviting members to attend our lessons with her. I believed I was experienced enough to handle all of her questions and doubts by myself.

After several more lessons, I could tell things were only getting worse. Humbling myself, I called our most doctrine-savvy member and asked him if he would be willing to attend our next lesson. I knew this next lesson would be a make-or-break lesson for Feng. The member accepted the invitation to join our lesson after I changed the lesson time to fit his busy schedule.

The day of the lesson came, and immediately following our opening prayer, Feng launched into her typical stream of questions and doubts. Soon our member had completely taken over the lesson and was talking through differences between Buddhism and Christianity that were far beyond my knowledge. I knew a little bit about Buddhism, but nothing compared to the locals. Thirty minutes later, my companion and I left for our next appointment, but our member stayed behind for two hours to resolve all of Feng's concerns.

Later that night, we received a text from Feng confirming her baptismal date. Two weeks later, she was baptized and now serves as the Gospel Principles teacher in Sichuan, China. Had I not humbled myself and invited a member to Feng's lesson that day, I'm not sure we would have ever had another lesson with her.

Feng, circled, building friendships with the ward members

SOMETIMES MEMBERS DON'T LIKE MISSIONARY WORK

In many of the places you serve, you will have some members that already love missionary work, but what do you do with the members or wards that don't? How do you help them catch the excitement? In these hard situations, it's key to serve the members and then find your own people to teach so they can see that the field is white. Finally, give the members some responsibility.

MATTHEW

I will never forget the Woodberry Ward and the change in the hearts of the members there. I had just been transferred into the ward, and the members told me they had just lost their "favorite elders" who had been serving there for the last eight months. We were the two "new guys," and our ideas about missionary work didn't seem to fit with what the ward expected, that missionaries do missionary work, while members attend church. It was clear that our energy for member missionary work was not welcome, and the ward didn't seem too thrilled about any of our changes. We had one or two members who seemed excited to work with us, but overall, we got a lot of "You can't do it like that, Elder." It was frustrating. For six weeks we pushed, pulled, and pushed some more. We tried to set up appointments with the members so we could get to know them, but many of them wouldn't let us come to their houses. At one point, the ward mission leader even told us that many of the members did not like us.

Not knowing what else to do, my companion and I began serving harder than we knew was possible. We prayed diligently that the members' hearts would soften. We slowly began finding our own people to bring to church. The members started to take notice of our "success."

As the weeks went on, more and more of the members started letting us come to their homes, because they noticed how hard we were working. We took our member lessons as seriously as any other lesson and made sure they felt the Spirit. Whether it was through a video we showed them, a song we sang them, the doctrine we taught, or the small success we were having through our own finding efforts, the members of the ward began to trust us.

Once we began to gain their trust, we didn't stop there. We started asking them to be missionaries. We encouraged members to talk to people on the street with us as we were walking to lessons and then had them invite people to be baptized in those same lessons. We sang hymns with members to strangers near public train stations and tried our best to have a member with us all day every day. Once we started giving members responsibilities and lifting them out of their comfort zones, their excitement for the work exploded.

Soon, it didn't feel like the members disliked us. We developed deep and lasting relationships with many of them. Others started noticing that the members who helped us the most seemed to be the happiest. We started inviting members to share their missionary experiences in testimony meetings, and soon missionary work was the topic of every meeting. What at first had been an inch-by-inch fight for any member to let us in their door had become an explosion of members taking initiative to spread the gospel. The attitude of the entire ward had completely changed. With the help of members, just a few weeks later, we got to be part of four baptisms, and we reactivated several more people.

It was the greatest change in attitude toward missionary work that I had seen in my entire mission. Looking back, what it came down to was all the extra people we talked to on the street, the members we served, the awkward moments in ward council when we asked people to change, and the love for our Savior.

I've learned that sometimes members just need to experience missionary work firsthand, because they don't fully understand what missionary work is or how to do it. With the right combination of faith in Christ, hard work, positivity, and service, you can mobilize an entire branch or ward of member missionaries. Without them, it's just you and your companion versus everyone. And that's no fun.

MEMBER REFERRALS

On the inside back cover of *Preach My Gospel*, there is a list of "Remember This" points that sum up all the most important principles from *Preach My Gospel*. To be more direct, if God had one list of bullet points to teach modern-day missionaries effective missionary skills, this would be it.

If you look closely, there is only one bullet point that is emphasized: "Ask for referrals from *everyone*!"

We've talked about asking strangers to refer their friends, but what about referrals from the members of the Church?

DAKOTA AND MATTHEW

I had been serving in the Tolle Ward for three months when Matthew was transferred into the ward to be my companion.

It was our first Sunday together, and we started planning our day. We began setting goals and making plans to receive referrals from members and less active members.

I looked with uncertainty at Matthew. I had been struggling to get any referrals from the members in this ward.

Matthew thought for a second and then smiled across the desk at me, clearly brewing some ingenious idea. "Well, tomorrow is my first Sunday, so I'll ask the bishop if I can introduce myself over the pulpit. Also, I'm sure you'll be introducing me to everyone in the ward, right?"

"Yeah, of course!" I responded, still unclear at what he was getting at.

"Well, when I introduce myself, I'll make sure to bring the Spirit into the room. They'll feel my energy for missionary work, and then when you introduce me to the members, we can just ask everyone if they know anyone they could invite to come unto Christ."

Is this guy serious? I thought. *His best idea is just to ask everyone to refer their friends? Where is the genius in that?* I was expecting some intricate plan to visit and share some life-changing message with the members in their homes. However, not wanting to drown out his "greenie-fire," I consented to his plain vanilla idea to just ask everyone for their friends.

A few hours later during sacrament meeting, Matthew bore a powerful testimony as he introduced himself, and the Spirit was clearly felt by all. (Note: When you have the opportunity to introduce yourself for the first time, don't just stand up and say, "Oh, hi! My name is Elder Boring, and I'm from Monotone, Montana" and then sit down. Stand with energy and make sure the members know who you are and why you are there.) In his introduction, Matthew also set the stage for our referral rampage by forewarning the members that when he met them he would, without hesitation, ask them to refer their friends or discuss other ways they could get involved in the Lord's work. It was a good start, but I was still skeptical.

After sacrament meeting, I began introducing Matthew to all the members. Two hours later, we had seventeen referrals, fifteen more than we had the entire previous week.

While I had gotten caught up in the intricacies of trying to first develop relationships with the members before helping them do missionary work, Matthew reminded me that often relationships with the members are made through doing missionary work together. Members expect missionaries to do missionary work. You don't have to beat around the bush.

MEMBERS WANT TO BE NATURAL

Simply asking members for referrals is a start, but encouraging members to naturally share the gospel in ways they feel comfortable will increase the "reaping" by much more. Most members want to share the gospel and their faith in Jesus Christ with others, but they feel awkward or unsure about how.

Elder Uchtdorf stated, "There are roughly seven and a half billion people in the world, compared to some sixteen million members of The Church of Jesus Christ of Latter-day Saints . . . Wherever you are on this earth, there are plenty of opportunities to share the good news of the gospel of Jesus Christ with people you meet, study with, and live with or work and socialize with" ("Missionary Work: Sharing What Is in Your Heart, *Ensign*, May 2019). Elder Uctdorf then went on to invite members to help those around them to "come and see." This is where you can help. You can encourage members to use a specific activity, media platform, or church service to connect with those who are prepared to receive the gospel. This process can go many ways. Here are a few examples:

- **ACTIVITIES.** Help members identify upcoming activities that would be natural for them to invite specific people to. For instance, if they have friends interested in music, they could invite them to a choir performance during sacrament meeting. Or, if they have friends who enjoy sports, perhaps their son or daughter could invite another youth to their Church basketball or soccer game. No matter what idea it is, you can help the members pray for guidance, set a time for when they will act, and, if needed, even role play the invitation. (Note: If your area has no activities in the near future, meet with your branch or ward leadership and ask how you can help facilitate interesting and different activities: ward open houses, temple grounds visits, English classes, cultural nights, sporting events, service projects or barbecues.)

- **MEDIA.** You can utilize many forms of media in helping members share the gospel. Using books or pamphlets like the Book of Mormon, informational pamphlets, websites like comeuntochrist.org, or social media can serve many types of needs. Giving a Book of Mormon to a friend or family member can seem daunting, but if it's prefaced with initial activities and experiences, this too can be natural.

- **CHURCH.** Each week at church, different people are giving prayers, talks, or musical performances. They are teaching lessons, bringing bread, and doing many other things. (See Clayton M. Christensen, *The Power of Everyday Missionaries*, 38–47.) Work with local leadership and meet with members of your ward or branch to help them understand how to invite others to come hear them speak, teach a portion of their lesson, contribute bread, or simply come and experience worshipping with them. Help members decide *when* they will invite, and, if needed, help them role play *how* they will invite.

DAKOTA

I was thirteen years old and had just started going to Boy Scouts more regularly. One day, one of my basketball coaches was complaining about how his son's Boy Scout troop wasn't doing enough. They were "lame," he said.

Without even thinking, I blurted out, "Well coach, we have a Boy Scout troop at our church. You are welcome to join. I think it's awesome."

I didn't think anything of it, but soon enough, my coach and his son were attending our Church's Boy Scout troop and were heavily involved. A year later, my coach and his wife were baptized and later sealed in the temple.

From my current missionary perspective, I wish I had thought to involve myself in teaching them the gospel, but that simple invitation to the Boy Scout troop was enough to naturally bring them to the Church.

Dakota's basketball coach, center, and his son, left, with Dakota, right, at a Boy Scout activity

THE GOLD MINE

Elder Brent H. Nielsen, the executive director of the Missionary Department, termed the group of less active and part-member families as the "gold mine" (fireside, Singapore Mission, 2015). These people are "gold," because they have already been exposed to the restored gospel through the Church or their family members.

They have already glimpsed the light of the gospel, so coming back to the fold or joining for the first time is more feasible.

Let's put ourselves in their shoes for a minute. Would you be more willing to hear the gospel from two random strangers who knock on your door or the missionaries from your mother's church after watching a new light come into her life from the gospel? The latter, of course!

In addition, active members tend to have mostly active member friends. It's counterintuitive, but the best sources of referrals are often the least-involved members.

MATTHEW

Elder Barn and I had been doing our best to talk with everyone. "Everyone," we learned, didn't just mean strangers on the streets but included active and less active members. We also began going through the ward list to find and contact people who hadn't been seen in years.

"The Lim family is next," I said to Elder Barn. The inactive Lim family supposedly consisted of a husband, wife, and their three children, although none of them had been seen in years.

We decided to drop by their apartment unannounced in the early afternoon when we had no other immediate plans so we could walk and then talk with everyone along the way. After thirty minutes of talking with everyone while making our way to their apartment, we arrived. We knocked on the door and waited.

Before we could finish knocking the second time, the door swung open suddenly.

"Hello! Are you Mrs. Daisy Lim?" asked Elder Barn.

"I am Mrs. Lim, but my name is not Daisy," she retorted. "That is my husband's ex-wife. My name is Grace."

Elder Barn and I looked at each other awkwardly. Oops.

We then explained how we were missionaries from her husband's church and were there to help their family find more peace and happiness.

Having started the conversation out on the wrong note, I wasn't expecting much of a response, but suddenly Grace became super excited. "You guys can come back another day if you want! I don't know much about God, but my husband is stressed these days, and I really think this could help him. He gets home around 7:00 p.m. every day," she said.

Two days later, we came back and began teaching the new Mr. and Mrs. Lim. Grace was from China and knew nothing about God, but she did know one thing: she wanted a happy family.

Within two weeks, Grace had read the entire Book of Mormon, and in another two weeks, she had read it again. As we taught about specific doctrine, she would often relate to us, "Oh yes! I read about that in the Book of Mormon this week!"

Within a month, Grace was baptized and reading the Doctrine and Covenants. Mr. Lim, although progressing a bit slower, was well on his way to overcoming his problems too. Their children began attending Primary, and it was clear that Grace had found the happy family she was looking for.

Mr. and Mrs. Lim were part of the gold mine. By focusing on less active and part-member families, you can reactivate members by helping them teach their non-member friends and family. In this way, they can strengthen their own testimonies while simultaneously helping their friends and family members as well.

Matthew and Elder Barn with the Lim family and a few members

Some of the people you baptize will go inactive. No matter what you do or how prepared you believe someone is for baptism, you can't take away someone's agency. We both have had many converts go inactive, but had we understood how to utilize members better, navigate the gold mine, and make sure we had members present at all our lessons, so many more of our converts would be active today. Before our missions, we knew members were important, but we didn't really understand how. Now you know how, and you have a chance to do better.

CHALLENGE #9

INVITE ONE PERSON TO COME TO AN ACTIVITY, READ A SCRIPTURE, OR ATTEND CHURCH

HELPFUL SUGGESTIONS

- Ask the missionaries if you can be a designated member who fellowships someone they are teaching (this means you will sit with them at church, be their friend, help answer their questions, etc.).

- Make a list of what has kept you from doing missionary work now as a member. How can you help the members of your future area overcome those things?

- Study the "Sister Susan Fulcher Case Study" (see everydaymissionaries.org/loving-is-easy-sister-susan-fulcher/#.Xpzn8i2ZN3Y).

CHAPTER 10

YOUR MISSION IS THE MTC FOR YOUR LIFE

DAKOTA

My mission has been the Missionary Training Center for my life in many ways. Post-mission, during my junior and senior years in college, I interviewed with companies such as Google, Apple, and Tesla. Having what most people would consider an outstanding engineering education, I believed most companies would focus on engineering questions in my interviews. However, the majority of the questions I was asked centered on my mission experience. Additionally, when I had to introduce myself at career events and began networking for jobs, unlike other students who hadn't served missions, I immediately thrived using all the same skills talked about in this book.

What I've since realized is that the emotional, social, and mental skills gained from a mission are irreplaceable. So when you think about giving up on your mission, don't. The payoff is too high. Not only will you see miracles and come to know Christ, but you will also develop collaboration, adaptability, and time management skills amidst a foreign environment (whether you serve foreign or not), with all different types of people and personalities. In my experience, these are the skills that companies and institutions value the most.

MATTHEW

When I got home from my mission, I wanted to continue to serve people around the world. I decided to start a nonprofit organization named MAJI, with a goal to train young men and women to be future leaders through service. We accomplish this by teaching them how to set goals and make plans related to how many people they want to serve, how to talk with strangers in order to gain funding for service projects, and how to recruit the volunteers who make the service possible. We are teaching young men and women how to be service missionaries.

As for my career, like Dakota, the soft skills I gained on my mission shaped what I want to do for the rest of my life. Since I was a little kid, I had always planned on and dreamed of being a doctor, but soon after my mission, I came to the realization that my passion for helping people around the world could be fulfilled through other career paths. Understanding how to listen, lead others, and problem solve has led me to jobs in strategy consulting. I'm not saying you shouldn't be a doctor, but rather that serving a mission will help you learn more about who you are in a divine sense and in terms of a career.

Currently, I work part time for The Church of Jesus Christ of Latter-day Saints' Missionary Department as a consultant for the missionary strategy team to solve the mission force's largest problems. Without my mission, I don't know where I would be today (and I don't want to know).

RETURNED MISSIONARIES CAN STILL DO MISSIONARY WORK?

The purpose of this book is to help you have fun doing missionary work. However, if you're genuine about it, you'll come home and continue to have an eternity of fun sharing the gospel.

We frequently hear returned missionaries say, "Oh, my mission converts? I have no idea how they are doing. I haven't talked to them in years." When you come home, please don't do that. Make sure you keep in contact with them. They need your help and support for the rest of their lives. In fact, the Prophet has instructed us to keep in contact with our converts (see *Preach My Gospel*, 128). This doesn't mean you need to be their best friend for life, and you'll definitely have other priorities once you come home, but make sure you send them an encouraging note or give them a phone call every once in awhile.

In addition, when you come home from your mission, you are at the peak of your missionary skills. You have just spent two years or eighteen months of your life developing the skills in this book and more. Make sure to put them to good use. We have had our most impactful missionary experiences after returning home from our missions.

MATTHEW

When I first returned home from my mission, I made a goal to be part of a baptism every year for the rest of my life. After praying one day, I decided that I wanted to share the gospel with my best friend from high school and felt prompted that now was the time. So I talked with him and shared my thoughts and feelings for the gospel. However, just like many times on the mission, I was rejected.

I felt I was supposed to talk to him, but soon after, I realized that it was actually his sister who was prepared to come unto Christ. Immediately, I invited her to meet with the missionaries, and she accepted. For months, we met with several different sets of missionaries, working on overcoming challenges and helping her gain a true testimony of the gospel.

Six months later, I had the privilege of baptizing my best friend's sister. It was undoubtedly one of the greatest missionary moments of my life. It's been three years since I've been home from my mission, and God has still blessed me to be a part of a baptism every year.

Tell God that you want to be a part of His work, and then do all you can to do so. We guarantee that if you do this, He will allow you to continue to work with Him. This isn't two years or eighteen months and out. This is eternity. An eternity of fun!

Matthew's best friend's sister at her baptism

DAKOTA

Like Matthew, some of my greatest converts also came after my mission. During my mission, I had set one particular goal with God to help an entire family be baptized. Although I baptized many people on my mission, I was never able to see that prayer come to fruition.

That all changed when I met John and his family six months after returning from my mission.

John was a forty-year-old man from China who moved to Boston with his wife and daughter for work. While in Boston, he felt inspired to search for a Christian church where he could worship. All he found, however, were services held in English, which were difficult for him to understand.

Frustrated, he began searching for what he called "a Chinese-speaking American missionary" who could guide him to a church service held in Chinese. He had no luck asking around, so one night, he prayed and asked God for help. He felt inspired to be a taxi driver so he could meet more Christian people, so he signed up and immediately started driving.

Three weeks later, I took John's taxi.

On that taxi ride, he was pleasantly surprised that I could speak Chinese and that I had been a church missionary. I invited him to church, and soon he and his family began coming to our Chinese branch in Boston. A few months later, John, his wife, and his only daughter were all baptized.

A year later, I had the chance to officiate their living endowment session in Chinese and act as a witness at their family's sealing in the Boston Temple.

Dakota with John and his family after their family sealing in the Boston Massachusetts Temple

After being home from my mission for over a year, God answered a prayer I had almost entirely forgotten about, a prayer I had concluded He didn't see fit to answer or just didn't listen to. Some of you might feel that God hasn't answered your prayer, that He isn't listening to your questions, or that He doesn't seem to be there at all. But I am here to promise you that He will answer. He does care. And He is there for you.

To quote Isaiah: "For my thoughts are not your thoughts, neither are your ways my ways" (Isaiah 55:8). And, might I add, "Neither is your time my time."

CHRIST'S *WHY*

You'll often hear that the mission is not about you. It's about Christ. However, in reality, He is because we are. Without us, Jesus Christ is left purposeless. So yes, the mission is about Jesus Christ, but it's also about you.

Jesus Christ doesn't need you to baptize people. He could certainly do it by himself, given His omnipotence, but He needs you in his corner. He needs you to come to know Him. We are Christ's *why*.

"Christ doesn't just want people in the Church. He wants the Church in people. He doesn't just want people to come to Him. He wants them to become like Him—a process that takes place 7 days a week, 52 weeks a year, and throughout all the years of our lives" (Brad Wilcox, *The 7-day Christian*).

People often complain about how long the name of the Church is, but without "of Latter-day Saints," you are leaving out half of the picture: us! The Church is meaningless without us! His children! His want-to-be saints! Even Jesus's prophesied name, "Emmanuel," literally means "God with us" (Matthew 1:23). Alone, Jesus Christ accomplished an amazing feat, being the first perfect person to live on earth, suffering every temptation, sickness, and sin ever known by mankind. But together, with us, He continues to work miracles.

Our mission president once taught us, "The gospel is individual. If you were the only person on earth, God still would have sent His Son." However, take that one person off the earth and there seems to be no need for a Savior.

You'll often hear that when you come home from your mission you'll feel the Spirit less. However, when you take the sacrament each week, the blessing doesn't say you'll feel the Spirit "sometimes," or "on your mission," or "when you're reading your scriptures." No! It says *always* (Moroni 4:3; emphasis added). God knew "by the sweat of your brow" you must work the days of your life, but He still promises us that we will have the Spirit with us always (Genesis 3:19, NIV). After your mission, it might be harder, but the promise is still the same.

When we started this book, we told you that its purpose is to help you have fun doing missionary work. However, the real purpose of this book is to help you *serve God*. With a firm testimony and the skills in this book, we hope you soon come to understand and experience the *fun* of serving God.

> For whosoever will save his life shall lose it: and whosoever will lose his life for my sake shall find it. For what is a man profited, if he shall gain the whole world, and lose his own soul? (Matthew 7:7–8)

We testify that Heavenly Father and Jesus Christ live. They know *Their* why. They are perfectly obedient. They work with and help "hard companions." They always have the Spirit with them. They choose an awesome attitude. They set S.M.A.R.T. goals and make specific plans. They have become master teachers, and They *love* missionary work. Their entire purpose is "to bring to pass the immortality and eternal life of man" (Moses 1:39).

We testify that They have a ton of fun doing *just* that.

You can and will too.

CHALLENGE #10

SET GOALS TO DO MISSIONARY WORK AS A RETURNED MISSIONARY AND STAY CONNECTED WITH YOUR CONVERTS.

HELPFUL SUGGESTIONS

- Make a list of all your converts, less active members helped, etc., and make plans to keep in contact with them.

- Read "Find the Lambs, Feed the Sheep" by President Gordon B. Hinckley, *Ensign*, May 1999.

- Read "The Returned Missionary," L. Tom Perry, *Ensign*, Nov. 2001.

PLEASE MESSAGE US WITH QUESTIONS OR SUCCESS STORIES.
EMAIL: THEMODERNDAYMISSIONARIES@GMAIL.COM
INSTAGRAM: @MODERNDAYMISSIONARIES
FACEBOOK: @MODERNDAYMISSIONARIES

BIBLIOGRAPHY

Adjusting to Missionary Life. Salt Lake City: The Church of Jesus Christ of Latter-day Saints, 2013.

A Successful Missionary, ldsinfobase.net/rh/missn/success.html. Accessed April 16, 2020.

Ballard, M. Russell. Talk given to Salt Lake Area Young Adults, Oct. 18, 1981. (See *Preach My Gospel*, printed edition.)

Barnes, Ted. "How to Never Have a Boring Church Class Ever Again." *New Era*, January 2013. (See churchofjesuschrist.org/study/new-era/2013/01/how-to-never -have-a-boring-church-class-ever-again?lang=eng. Accessed April 16, 2020.)

Benson, Ezra Taft. *Teachings of Ezra Taft Benson*. Salt Lake City: Bookcraft, 1988.

Brigham Young University firesides and devotionals. See BYU Speeches at speeches.edu. byu. Accessed April 16, 2020.

Brooks, David. *Road to Character*. New York: Random House, 2015.

Christensen, Clayton M. *The Power of Everyday Missionaries*. Salt Lake City: Deseret Book, 2013.

Cleveland Clinic. "Stress." (See my.clevelandclinic.org/health/articles/11874-stress, 2015. Accessed April 16, 2020.)

Covey, Stephen R. *First Things First*. New York: Free Press (Simon and Schuster), 1996.

Dew, Sheri L. "The 2 Sentences That Changed President Gordon B. Hinckley's Life Forever," *LDS Living* magazine, May 16, 2017. (Excerpted from *Go Forward with Faith: The Biography of Gordon B. Hinckley*. Salt Lake City: Deseret Book, 1996.)

Einstein, Albert. *The World As I See It*. Hawthorne, CA: BN Publishing, 2005 (1949).

Ensign magazine of The Church of Jesus Christ of Latter-day Saints.

Eyring, Henry B., and Jeffrey R. Holland. Face to Face, Mar. 4, 2017. (See churchofjesuschrist.org/church/events/face-to-face-with-president-eyring-and -elder-holland?lang=eng. Accessed April 16, 2020.)

Friend magazine of The Church of Jesus Christ of Latter-day Saints.

"Fundamentals from *Preach My Gospel*: Teach People Not Lessons," missionary .lds.org/content/dam/mportal/mission-presidents/pdfs/other-training/ Fundamentals%20of%20PMG%20Lessons-eng.pdf.

Hinckley, Gordon B. *Teachings of Gordon B. Hinckley* (Salt Lake City: Deseret Book, 2016.

Carnegie, Dale. *How to Win Friends and Influence People in the Digital Age*. New York: Simon and Schuster, 2012.

Huff Post. "Why You're Instructed to Put Oxygen Masks on Yourself First," huffpost .com/entry/why-youre-instructed-to-p_b_11201778, 2017. Accessed April 16, 2020.

Joseph Smith—History in the Pearl of Great Price.

Journal of Discourses. 26 vols. London: Latter-day Saints' Book Depot, 1854–86.

Lewis, C. S. *Mere Christianity*. San Francisco: HarperOne (Harper-Collins), 2009.

_____. *The Weight of Glory*. San Francisco: HarperOne (Harper-Collins), 2001.

McKinley, Michael. *Am I Really a Christian?* Wheaton, IL: Crossway, 2011.

Missionary Standards for Disciples of Jesus Christ, churchofjesuschrist.org/study/ manual/missionary-standards-for-disciples-of-jesus-christ?lang=eng. Accessed April 16, 2020.

Nielson, Brent H. Fireside, 2015.

Moral Stories, moralstories.org/frog-hot-water/. Accessed April 16, 2020.

Morgenegg, Ryan, and Kevin P. Miller. *Three Ways to Keep Conflict from Becoming Contention*, churchofjesuschrist.org/church/news/three-ways-to-keep-conflict -from-becoming-contention?lang=eng. Accessed April 16, 2020.

New Era magazine, The Church of Jesus Christ of Latter-day Saints.

Packer, Boyd K. As quoted in the commencement remarks of Don R. Clarke at BYU-Idaho, July 20, 2012; thechurchnews.com/archives/2012-07-27/byu-idaho-a-bountiful-harvest-50603. Accessed April 21, 2020.

_____. *Mine Errand from the Lord*. Salt Lake City: Deseret Book, 2008.

Preach My Gospel. Salt Lake City: The Church of Jesus Christ of Latter-day Saints, printed edition, 2004.

Ricks College firesides and devotionals. See web.byui.edu/DevotionalsAndSpeeches/. Accessed April 16, 2020.

Salt Lake City Weekly. "Solarsuit: SLC band release debut album before leaving on LDS missions," April 24, 2014. See cityweekly.net/utah/solarsuit /Content?oid=2368475. Accessed April 16, 2020.

Smith, Hank R. Twitter, twitter.com/hankrsmith/status/ 1121099964329783296, April 24, 2019. Accessed April 21, 2020.

Smith, Joseph. *History of The Church of Jesus Christ of Latter-day Saints*. Edited by B. H. Roberts. 2d ed. rev., 7 vols. Salt Lake City: The Church of Jesus Christ of Latter-day Saints, 1932–51.

Smith, Joseph. *Teachings of Presidents of the Church: Joseph Smith*. Salt Lake City: The Church of Jesus Christ of Latter-day Saints, 2007.

Stallings, Mary. Come Follow Me Daily, instagram.com/p/B8FDXYnBDRr /?utm_source=ig_web_copy_link, February 2, 2020. Accessed April 21, 2020.

Talmage, James E. *Jesus the Christ*. Salt Lake City: Deseret Book, 1915–2004.

True to the Faith. Salt Lake City: The Church of Jesus Christ of Latter-day Saints, 2004.

Wilcox, Brad. *Changed through His Grace*. Salt Lake City: Deseret Book, 2017.

_____. *The 7-Day Christian*, Salt Lake City: Shadow Mountain (Deseret Book), 2016.

Wooden, John. *A Lifetime of Observations and Reflections On and Off the Court*. Chicago, IL: Contemporary Books, 1997.

ABOUT THE AUTHORS

DAKOTA

Dakota Pierce was born in Southern California in 1995. As he grew up, he dreamed of becoming an astronaut, who would one day bless the first sacrament on Mars. To pursue this dream, Dakota moved to Boston, Massachusetts, where he attended the Massachusetts Institute of Technology (MIT), studying Aeronautical Engineering and playing shooting guard for the varsity basketball team.

After his freshmen year at MIT, Dakota served a mission in Singapore and Malaysia and learned to speak Mandarin Chinese. Upon returning home, Dakota first worked for NASA before deciding to put his space dreams on hold to utilize his mission language and skills for Apple Inc. by managing production of their new products in China.

MATTHEW

Matthew Spurrier was born in Utah in 1995. After high school, he served a mission in Singapore and Malaysia, speaking Malay and learning conversational Mandarin. Whether playing keyboard for the Spotify Indie Pop Top 100 band Solarsuit; performing brain surgery on monkeys for visual research; or founding the nonprofit organization MAJI, with the goal of inspiring youth to become future service leaders, Matthew loves having fun.

During college, he made it a goal to become the world's best member missionary and has a ways to go. Matthew graduated from the University of Utah in health policy. He is currently working as a consultant for Oliver Wyman. Matthew is happily married to the love of his life, Mackenzie.

Matthew and Dakota both served in the Singapore Mission (which includes Singapore and Malaysia) from 2014–16. They served together as companions for five months and are now lifelong best friends.

NOTES & IMPRESSIONS

NOTES & IMPRESSIONS

NOTES & IMPRESSIONS

NOTES & IMPRESSIONS